OUT AND ABOUT LONDON

BY

THOMAS BURKE

AUTHOR OF "LIMEHOUSE NIGHTS"
AND "NIGHTS IN LONDON"

Copyright © 2013 Read Books Ltd.
This book is copyright and may not be
reproduced or copied in any way without
the express permission of the publisher in writing

British Library Cataloguing-in-Publication Data
A catalogue record for this book is available from the
British Library

A Short Introduction to the History of London

London has been a major settlement since being founded by the Romans, who named it Londinium, two thousand years ago. As the capital city of England, it is also the country's most populous city, with its metropolitan area housing over thirteen million inhabitants and taking the crown of the most visited city in the world. At the centre of this, now gargantuan metropolis, is an area known as the City of London, covering only 2.9Km 2 – still contained within its medieval boundaries. Due to this peculiar quirk of history, 'the City of London' actually qualifies as the smallest city in England.

The first sizable conurbation appeared in the region in 43 AD, but only lasted seventeen years until it was ransacked and burned by the Iceni tribe led by Queen Boudica. Its next incarnation was more successful when in the second century AD it acted as the capital of the Roman province of Britannia – its population then swelled to sixty thousand. This settlement survived until the fifth century when it was largely abandoned due to the collapse of the Roman Empire. It was then the turn of the Anglo-Saxons to become the dominant force in the area, building it up into a major trade port by the mid seventh century. This success became very difficult to maintain as the following centuries found London's inhabitants having to defend themselves against an onslaught of Viking invasions and their subsequent occupation of much of the east and northern parts of England.

The City continued to grow throughout the Middle Ages, for the most part after the Battle of Hastings in 1066

AD and the conquest of the Normans. William, Duke of Normandy, was crowned in the newly finished Westminster Abbey and consolidated his presence by ordering the construction of the Tower of London and Westminster Hall. Over the next hundred years the central government of England became fixed in the area of the City of Westminster while the City of London, its neighbour, flourished into England's most populous city (as well as its commercial centre). This district grew and grew until the disastrous onset of the Black Death in the mid fourteenth century.

The Black Death resulted in a third of the City of London's inhabitants being lost to the pandemic. It was estimated to have killed over one hundred million people throughout Europe. This however, was not to be London's only catastrophe. The Great Plague of 1665 which killed 100,000 people was immediately followed by the Great Fire of London in 1666. This particularly devastating blaze swept through the central parts of the city, destroying many of the predominantly wooden buildings, all in all resulting in the loss of 13,200 houses, 87 parish churches, St. Paul's Cathedral and most of the city authority's buildings. The destruction was on a large scale, but London was not to be broken. Under the supervision of the surveyor Robert Hooke, a rebuilding programme was ordered and the city underwent a ten year period of reconstruction.

In the wake of this rebuilding some of the city's most iconic buildings and areas appeared, such as St Paul's Cathedral and the district of Mayfair. This bustling capital city became a hub for both business and culture, and the place to be for forward thinking academics. The famed scholar Samuel Johnson (1709-1784) once commented:

'You find no man, at all intellectual, who is willing to leave London. No, Sir, when a man is tired of London, he is tired of life; for there is in London all that life can afford.'

During the Victorian era London became the world's largest city as it gradually expanded to join up with the surrounding counties who operated under the banner of the London County Council. It was seen as a city of progress, and thousands flocked to be a part of the industrial and economic development. This sudden enlargement led to paralysing traffic congestion however, which required a novel solution. This resulted in the construction of the world's first underground rail network, a shining example of the engineering prowess of a nation on the up. Despite such success stories, the twentieth century brought with it a new adversary to deal with, the air raid. Although significant bombardments were made in the First World War, it was the Second World War that saw the catastrophic potential of this new aerial technology. The German Luftwaffe killed over thirty thousand inhabitants and reduced large tracts of the city to rubble. Before the war London reached its peak population at around 8.6 million in 1939, but following the conflict its numbers fell to an estimated 6.8 million in the 1980s.

London continues to be a hugely influential, cosmopolitan capital, and remains a hive of cultural innovation. It has a long and multi-faceted history and it is hoped that this brief introduction has inspired the reader to find out more.

1916

Lady, the world is old, and we are young.
  The world is old to-night and full of tears
And tumbled dreams, and all its songs are sung,
  And echoes rise no more from the tombed years.
Lady, the world is old, but we are young.

Once only shines the mellow moon so fair;
  One speck of Time is Love's Eternity.
Once only can the stars so light your hair,
  And the night make your eyes my psaltery.
Lady, the world is old. Love still is young.

Let us take hand ere the swift moment end.
  My heart is but a lamp to light your way,
My song your counsellor, my love your friend,
  Your soul the shrine whereat I kneel and pray.
Lady, the world grows old. Let us be young.

T. B.

CONTENTS

	PAGE
ROUND THE TOWN, 1917	3
BACK TO DOCKLAND	30
CHINATOWN REVISITED	40
SOHO CARRIES ON	58
OUT OF TOWN	69
IN SEARCH OF A SHOW	82
VODKA AND VAGABONDS	89
THE KIDS' MAN	113
CROWDED HOURS	123
SATURDAY NIGHT	134
RENDEZVOUS	140
TRAGEDY AND COCKNEYISM	148
MINE EASE AT MINE INN	155
RELICS	168
ATTABOY!	176

OUT AND ABOUT LONDON

ROUND THE TOWN, 1917

IT was a lucid, rain-washed morning—one of those rare mornings when London seems to laugh before you, disclosing her random beauties. In every park the trees were hung with adolescent tresses, green and white and yellow, and the sky was busy with scudding clouds. Even the solemn bricks had caught something of the sudden colour of the day, and London seemed to toss in its long, winter sleep and to take the heavy breaths of the awakening sluggard.

I turned from my Fleet Street window to my desk, took my pen, found it in good working order, and put it down. I was hoping that it would be damaged, or that the ink had run out; I like to deceive myself with some excuse for not working. But on this occasion none presented itself save the call of the streets and the happy aspect of things, and I made these serve my purpose. With me it is always thus. Let there come the first sharp taste of Spring in the February air and I am demoralized. Away with labour. The sun is shining. The sky is bland. There are seven hundred square miles of London in which Adventure is shyly lurking for those who will seek her out. What about it? So I drew five pounds from the cash-box, stuffed it into my waistcoat-pocket, and let myself loose, feeling, as the phrase goes, that I didn't care if it snowed. And as I walked, there rose in my heart a silly song, with no words and no tune; or, if any words, something like—how does it go?—

> Boys and girls, come out to play—
> Hi-ti-hiddley-hi-ti-hay!

But the fool is bent upon a twig. I found the boys preoccupied and the girls unwearied in warwork. One good comrade of the highways and byways had married a wife; and therefore he could not come. Another had bought a yoke of oxen, and must needs go and prove them as though they were a problem of Euclid. Luckily, I ran against Caradoc Evans, disguised in a false beard, in order to escape the fury of the London Welshmen, and looking like the advance agent of a hard winter. Seeing my silly, harkhalloa face, he inquired what was up. I explained that I was out for a day's amusement—the first chance I had had since 1914. Whereupon, he ran me into a little place round the corner, and bought me an illicit drink at an hour when the minatory finger of Lord d'Abernon was still wagging; and informed me with tears in the voice, and many a "boy bach," and "old bloke," and "indeed," that this was the Year of Grace 1917, and that London was not amusing.

It was not until the third drink that I discovered how right he was. As a born Cockney, living close to London every minute of my life, I had not noticed the slow change in the face and soul of London. I had long been superficially aware that something was gone from the streets and the skies, but the feeling was no more definite than that of the gourmet whose palate hints that the cook has left something—it cannot say what—out of the soup. It was left for the swift perception of the immigrant Welshman to apprise me fully of the truth. But once it was presented to me, I saw it too clearly. My search for amusement, I knew then, was at an end, and what had promised to be an empurpling of the town seemed like to degenerate into a spelling-bee. Of course, I might have gone back to my desk; but the Spring had worked too far into my system to allow even a moment's consideration of that alternative. There remained nothing to do but to wander, and to pray for a glimpse of that tempestuous petticoat of youth that deserted us in 1914. It was a forlorn pursuit: I knew I would never touch its hem.

I never did. I wandered all day with Caradoc bach, and we did this and we did that, while I strove to shake from my shoulders the bundle of dismay that seemed fastened there. The young men having gone to war, the streets were filled with middle-aged women of thirty, in short skirts, trying to attract the aged satyrs, the only men that remained, by pretending to be little girls. At mid-day, that hour when, throughout London, you may hear the symphony of swinging gates and creaking bolts, we paid hurried calls at the old haunts. They were either empty or filled with new faces. Rule's, in Maiden Lane, was deserted. The Bodega had been besieged by, and had capitulated to, the Colonial army. Mooney's had become the property of the London Irish. The vociferous rehearsal crowds had decamped from the Bedford Head, and left it to strayed and gloomy Service men, who cared nothing for its traditions; and Yates's Wine Lodge, the home of the blue-chinned laddies looking for a shop, was filled with women war-workers.

Truly, London was no more herself. The word carried no more the magical quality with which of old time it was endued. She was no more the intellectual centre, or the political centre, or the social centre of the world. She was not even an English city, like Leeds or Sheffield or Birmingham. She was a large city with a population of nondescript millions.

This I realized more clearly when, a week or so after our tour, an American, whom I was conducting round London, asked me to show him something typically English. I couldn't. I tried to take him to an English restaurant. There was none. Even the old chop-houses, under prevailing restrictions, were offering manufactured food like spaghetti and disguised offal. I turned to the programmes of the music-halls. Here again England was frozen out. There were comedians from France, jugglers from Japan, conjurers from China, trick-cyclists from Belgium, weight-lifters from Australia, buck-dancers from America, and . . . England, with all thy faults I love thee still; but do take a bit of interest in yourself. A stranger, arriving from overseas, might suppose that the war was over, and that London was in the hands of the conquerors. This impression he might receive from a single glance at our streets. The Strand at the moment of writing is blocked for pedestrian traffic by Australians and New Zealanders; Piccadilly Circus belongs to the Belgians and the French; and the Americans possess Belgravia. Canadian cafeterias are doing good business round Westminster; French coffee-bars are thriving in the Shaftesbury Avenue district; Belgian restaurants occupy the waste corners around Kingsway; and two more Chinese restaurants have lately been opened in the West End.

The common Cockney seemed to walk almost fearfully about his invaded streets, hardly daring to be himself or talk his own language. Apart from the foreign tongues, which always did annoy his ear, foul language now assailed him from every side: "no bon," "napoo," "gadget," "camouflaged," "buckshee," "bonza," and so on. This is not good slang. Good slang has a quality of its own—a bite and spit and fine expressiveness which do not belong to dictionary words. That is its justification—the supplying of a lacking shade of expression, not the supplanting of adequate forms. The old Cockney slang did justify itself, but this modern Army rubbish, besides being uncouth, is utterly meaningless, and might have been invented by some idiot schoolboy: probably was.

After some search, we found a quiet corner in a bar where the perverted stuff was not being talked, and there we gave ourselves to recalling the little joyous jags that marked the progress of other years. I was dipping the other night into a favourite bedside book of mine—here I'd like to put in a dozen pages on bedside books—a Social Calendar for 1909; a rich reliquary for the future historian; and was shocked on noting the number of simple festivals which are now ruled out of our monotonous year. Do you remember them? Chestnut Sunday at Bushey Park—City and Suburban—Derby and Oaks—Ascot Sunday at Maidenhead—Cup Tie at the Crystal Palace—Spring week-ends by the sea—evening taxi jaunts to Richmond and Staines—gay nights at the Empire and the adjoining bars—supper after the theatre—moonlight trips in the summer season down river to the Nore—polo at Ranelagh—cricket at Lord's and the Oval—the Boat Race—Henley week—Earl's Court and

White City Exhibitions, where one could finish the evening on the wiggle-woggle, as a final flicker. And now they have just delivered the most brutal blow of all. Having robbed us of our motors and our cheap railways, they have stolen away from the working-man his (and my) chiefest delight—the beanfeast wagonette. (How I would have loved to take Henry James on one of these jags.) The disappearance of this delight of the summer season is, at the moment, so acute and so personal a grief, that I cannot trust myself to speak of it. I must withdraw, and leave F. W. Thomas (of *The Star*) to deliver the valedictory address:—

This spells the death of yet another old English institution. One cannot go beanfeasting in traps and pony carts. There would be no room for the cornet man, and without his distended cheeks and dreadful harmony the picture would be incomplete.

That was a great day when we met at the works in the morning, all in our best clothes and squeaky boots, all sporting large buttonholes and cigars of the rifle-range brand.

With the yellow stone jars safely stowed under the seat and the cornet man perched at the driver's left hand, we started off. Usually the route lay through Shoreditch and Hackney to Clapton, and so to the green fields of the Lea Bridge Road.

For the first hour of the journey we were quiet, early-morningish, and a little reminiscent, recalling the glories of past beanfeasts. The cornet man tootled half-heartedly, with many rests and much licking of dry lips. Not until the "Greyhound" was passed did he get well under way, and then there was no stopping him. His face got redder and redder as he blasted his way through his repertoire; a feast of music covering the years between "Champagne Charlie" and Marie Lloyd.

At the end of the drive the horses were put up and baited, and the merry beanfeasters spread themselves and their melody through the glades of Loughton or High Beech, with cold roast beef and pickles at Queen Elizabeth's Hunting Lodge or the "Robin Hood."

And who does not remember that joyful homeward journey, with the cornet man, now ruddier than the cherry, blaring "Little Brown Jug" from well-oiled lungs, while behind him the revellers sang "As your hair grows whiter," and an accordion in the back seats bleated "The Miner's Dream."

As Herbert Campbell used to sing in the old days:—

> Then up I came with my little lot,
> And the air went blue for miles;
> The trees all shook and the copper took his hook,
> And down came all the tiles.

That was the real tit-bit of the beanfeast, the rollicking homeward drive, with the brake embowered in branches of trees raped from the Forest, and lit by swaying Chinese lanterns and great bunches of dahlias bought from the cottagers of Loughton, and Chingford.

One always took home a bunch of flowers from a beanfeast, and maybe a pint of shrimps for the missus, and some acorns for the youngsters, or a gilded mug.

The defunct brake had other uses than this. Sometimes it took parties of solemn old ladies in beads and black to an orgy of tea and cake in the grounds of the "Leg of Mutton" at Chadwell Heath. These were prim affairs. Mothers' Meeting from the little red church round the corner. They had no cornet, and the smiling parson rode in the seat assigned to Orpheus.

The youngsters, too, had their days—riotous days shrill with song and gay with coloured streamers, air-balloons and trumpets. How merrily they would bellow that they were "all a-going to Rye House, so 'Ip-ip-ip-ooray!'" though their destination was Burnham Beeches or Brickett Wood.

Rubber-neck parties of American tourists occasionally saw the sights of London from brakes and wagonettes; solemn people, who for all the signs of holiday they displayed might have been driving to Tyburn Tree.

But the real reason for the brake was the beanfeast with its attendant cornet man and its rubicund driver with his white topper and the little boys running behind and stealing rides on the back step. Until the war is over Epping will know them no more, and the nightingales of Fairlop Plain will sing to the moon undisturbed.

We lunched at the "Trocadero," where a friend on the staff put us in the right place and put before us the right food and the right wine. The rooms looked like a Service mess-room. Every guest looked like every other guest. Men and women alike had fallen victims to that devastating plague of uniforms, and all charm, all significance, had been obliterated by this murrain of khaki and blue serge. The suave curves of feminine dress had been ironed out by the harsh hand of the standardizer, and in their place we saw only the sullen lines of the Land Girls' rig making juts and points with the rigidities of the Women's Army Corps and Women's Police garb. The Vorticists ought to be thankful for the war. It accomplished in one stroke what, in 1914, they were feverishly attempting: it turned life into a wilderness of angles.

"Clothes," said Carlyle, "gave us individuality, distinction, social polity." He ought to see us now. Standard Bread, Standard Suits, Standard This, and Standard That. . . . The very word "standard" must now be so universally loathed by men who have managed to conceal from the controllers some remnants of character, that I wonder the *Evening Standard* manages to retain its popularity without a change of title. If standardizing really helped matters, nobody could complain; but can Dogberry aver that it does? Does it not, in practice, rather hinder than help? In railway carriages the bottlefed citizen girds against all this aimless interference with his daily life; but his protests are no more considerable than that of the victim in the melodrama: "Have a care, Sir Aubrey, have a care. You have ruined me sister. You have murdered me wife. You have cast me aged father into prison. You have seduced me son. You have sold up me home. But beware, Sir Aubrey, beware. I am a man of quick temper. *Don't go too far.*"

When we looked round the Trocadero, and we

remembered the bright company it once held, and then noted the tart aspect of the place under organization, we felt a little unwell, and dared to wonder why efficiency cannot walk with beauty and the zeal for victory go with grace and gladness. Had the marriage, we wondered, been tried by the authorities, and the parties proved to be so palpably incompatible? Or was it that they had been for ever sundered by some one who mistakes dullness for earnestness and ugliness for strength?

However, the rich scents of well-cooked offal, mingled with those of wine and Oriental tobacco, soothed us a little, and we achieved a brief loosening of the prevailing restraint, and allowed our thoughts to run without the chain. Our friend had dug from the depths of the cellar a fragrant Southern wine, true liquid sunshine, tinct with the odour of green seas; a rare bottle to which I made a chant-royal on the back of the menu, and, luckily for you, mislaid the thing, or it would be printed here. We talked freely; not brilliantly, but with just that touch of piquancy that stimulants and narcotics, rightly used, bestow upon the brain.

We lounged over coffee and liqueurs, and then

strolled up the Avenue and called at the establishment of " Mr. Francis Downman," that most discriminating and charming of wine-merchants— discriminating because he has given his life to the study of wines; charming because, away from his wine-cellars and in his true name, he is a novelist whose books, so lit with sparkle and espièglerie, have carried fair breezes into many a dusty heart. If you have ever visited that old Queen Anne House in Dean Street and glanced at " Mr. Downman's " Bulletins, you will realize at once that here is no ordinary vendor of wines. Wine to " Mr. Downman " is a serious matter. Opening a bottle is an exquisite ceremony; drinking is a sacrament. I once lunched with " Mr. Downman " in his cool Dutch kitchen " over the shop," and each course was lovingly cooked and served by his own hands, with suitable wines and liqueurs. It was a lesson in simple and courtly living. How pleasant the homes of England might be if our housewives would pay a little attention to correct kitchen and table amenities. " Mr. Downman " would be a public benefactor if he would open a School of Kitchen Wisdom where the little suburban wife might sit at his feet and learn of him. Yes, I know that there are many schools of cookery and housewifery, but these places are managed by people who only know how to cook. "Mr. Downman" would bring to the task all those little elegancies which make a dinner not merely satisfactory, but a refinement of joy. Feeding, like all functions of the human body, is a vulgar business anyway, but here is a man who can raise it to the dignity of a rite.

Further, he has shown us, in those "Bulletins," how to turn advertising into one of the minor arts. Perhaps of all the enormities which the nineteenth century perpetrated in its efforts to make life unbearable, the greatest was the debasing of trade. In the eighteenth century trade was a serene occupation, as you may see by glancing at the files of the old *Gentleman's Magazine, Mirror, Spectator,* where announcements of goods and merchandise were made in fine flowing English. Advertisement was then a matter of grace, of flourish and address; for people had leisure in which to receive gradual impressions. The merchants of that day did not scream at you; they sat with you over the fire, and held you in pleasant converse, sometimes, in their talk, throwing off some persiflage or apothegm that has become immortal. There was a Mr. George Farr, a grocer, *circa* 1750, who issued some excellent trade tickets from the "Beehive and Three Sugar Loaves"; little cards, embellished with dainty woodcuts that bring to mind an Elzevir bookplate; the pictures a sheer joy to look upon, the prose a delicate pomp of words that delights the ear. Then there were the trade cards of the Goldsmiths' and Silversmiths' Company of the eighteenth century, each one the production of a true artist (Hogarth did several), as well as the tobacco advertisements of the same period. In the latter case, not only were the cards works of art, but poetry was wooed and won for the cause. Near the old Surrey Theatre lived one John Mackey, who sang the praise of his wares in rhyme and issued playbills purporting to announce new tragedies under such titles as *My Snuff-Box, The Indian Weed, The True Friend, or Arrivals from Havannah, The Last Pinch*, and so on. The cabinet-makers of the eighteenth century also found time to indite delicious morsels of prose and prepare quaint and harmonious pictures for the delight of their patrons. Mr. Chippendale and Mr. Heppelwhite were most industrious in this direction, and the Society of Upholsterers and Cabinet Makers issued, in 1765, a work now very much sought after: *The Cabinet and Chair Makers' Real Friend and Companion.*

But then, snorting and hustling like a provincial alderman, in came the nineteenth century, with its gospel of Speed-up; and the result was that fair fields and stately streets scream harshly in your ears at every turn:—

DRINK BINGO.
It is the Best.

EAT DINKYDUX.
You'll hate it at First.

This sort of thing continued for many decades, when, happily, its potency became attenuated, and some genius discovered that people were not always responsive to screams; that, after all, the old way was better.

Thus literature returned and linked arms once again with trade. Partly, the circularizing dodge was responsible for this, since, in the circular, the bald statement was hardly good enough. It was found that subtle means must be employed if you are striving to catch a man's attention at the breakfast-table, when sleep still crawls like a slug about the brain and temper is uncertain. Nothing is so riling to the educated person as to have ungrammatical circulars dropped in his letter-box. Their effect is that he heartily detests the article advertised, not because he has tried it and found it wanting, but because of the split infinitive or the infirm phrase. So the whoop and the yell gave place to the full-flowered essay sprigged with the considered phrase. And to my mind the best of all contemporary efforts in this direction are "Mr. Downman's" "Bulletins," of which I have a complete set. Here a fastidious pen is delightfully employed; and not the pen only, but the taste of the book-lover. Indeed, they are lovable productions, having all the gracious response to the eye and the touch of Mr. Arthur Humphreys' anthologies of seventeenth-century poetry. Everything—format, type, paper, and Elian style—breathes an air of serendipity.

The first part of each "Bulletin" consists of a number of essays on questions pertaining to wine and wine-drinking; the second half is a catalogue of "Mr. Downman's" wines and their current prices, with specimen labels, which are such gentle harmonies of line and colour that one is tempted to start collecting them. " Mr. Downman" opens his addresses in the grand manner:—

My Lords, Reverend Fathers, Ladies and Gentlemen.

And if you love your Elia, then you must read " Mr. Downman " on Decanters and Decanting, On Corkscrews, On How to Drink Wine, On Bottling, On Patriotism and Wines, On the Suiting of Food to Wine, On Wines at Picnics. His sharp-flavoured prose, full of sly nuances and coquettish conceits, has all the tone of the best claret. Hear him on salads:—

> This is the time of salads. And a good salad means good oil. It also means good vinegar, or a fresh and juicy lime or lemon. Now the Almighty has given us better tools for salad-making than any wooden fork or spoon. In conditions of homely intimacy, a salad-maker, when all is ready, will wash his hands well and long as the moment approaches for serving the bowl. He will shun common or perfumed soaps, and will use nothing but a soap made from olive oil. Having dried his hands perfectly on a warm, clean towel, he will finally whisk the cup of dressing into homogeneity, will pour its contents over the salad, and will immediately proceed to wring the leaves in the liquid as a washerwoman wrings clothes in soapy water. (How horrid!) In doing this he will spoil the appearance of some of the leaves, but he will have a salad fit for the gods.

After sampling a noble Madeira in his cellar cool, in William and Mary Yard, we resumed our crawl, and in the black evening made a tour of other of the old places. At the Café de l'Europe, Mr. Jacobs, leader of the band, played for us a few old waltzes and morceaux reeking of the spirit of 1912; but even he did not handle the fiddle, or seem to care to handle it, in his old happy manner. Like the rest of us, I suppose, he felt that it wasn't worth while; it didn't matter. We called at the "Gambrinus," now owned by a Belgian; at the old "Sceptre," for a coupon's worth of boiled beef; and so to the Café Royal.

Here we received a touch or two from the old times. War has killed many lovely things, but, though it maim and break, it cannot wholly kill the things of the spirit, and in the "Royal" we found that art was still a living thing; ideas were still being discussed as though they mattered. Epstein and Augustus John, both in uniform, were there, and Austin Harrison had his usual group of poets. It was reassuring to see the old domino-playing Frenchmen, who seem part of the fixtures of the place, in their accustomed corner. The girls seemed to have packed away their affrighting futurist gowns, and were arrayed more soberly. That night they seemed to be more like human creatures, and less like deliberate Bohemians.

I am not overfond of the Café Royal, but it is one of the West End shows which visitors feel they must see; and when any provincial visitors wonder: " Why is the Café Royal? " I have one answer for them: " Henri Murger."

It is certain that, but for Murger, there would be no Chelsea and no Café Royal. That man has a lot to answer for. I doubt if any one man (I'm not including kings) has wrought so much havoc in young lives. He meant to warn youth of danger; he actually drove youth towards it.

Any discussion which seeks to name the most dangerous book in the world is certain to bring mention of Rousseau's *Confessions,* of Paine's *Age of Reason,* of Artzibashef's *Sanine,* of Baudelaire's *Fleurs de Mal,* and other works of subversive tendency. The one book which has really done more harm to young people than any other is seldom remembered in this connection. That book is *Scènes de la Vie de Bohême;* and it is dangerous, not that it contains a line of obscenity or blasphemy, not that it teaches evil as higher than good, but because it founded a cult and taught young people how to ruin their lives. Bohemianism has, of course, existed since the world began; rebels have always been; but it remained for Murger to find a name for it and make a cult of it. The dangers of this cult to young people lay not in its being an evil cult, but in its being perhaps as fine a cult as any of the world's great creeds: the cult of human sympathy and generosity. The Bohemian makes friends with all kinds and all creeds—sinners and saints, rich and poor; he cares nothing so long as they be kindly. And there lay the danger, for the blood of youth, freed from all restraint, was certain to overdo it. It became a cult of excess. Murger died, but he left behind him a very bitter legacy to the coming generation. As that legacy passed through the years it gathered various adhesions—such as Wilde's " In order to be an artist it is first necessary to ruin one's health," and Flaubert's " Nothing succeeds like excess "; so that very soon art colonies became things discredited, unpleasant to the nostrils of the righteous.

Murger himself saw the life very clearly, for he described it as " Vie gai et terrible "; and he takes no pains to present to us only the lighter, warmer side of it. He shows us everything; yet, so diabolical is his manner, that, even after passing the tragedy of the closing pages, the book and the life it pictures call to every one of us with song in his blood and the spirit of April in his heart.

It first appeared as a feuilleton in a Paris daily, and Murger, with characteristic insouciance, wrote his instalments only a few hours before the time when they were due for the printer; and when he was stumped for material, he invented a little story. Hence that singularly beautiful tale, slammed into the middle of the book—the Story of Francine's Muff—which forms the opening scene of Puccini's opera founded on the novel. The book has neither balance nor cohesion, and in this it catches its note from its theme. It is a cinematographic succession of scenes, tender and passionate and gay; swift and hectic. He invented and employed the picture-palace manner in literature before the picture-palace was even conceived. The very style is feverish, and from it one visualizes the desperately merry Bohemian slaving with pen and paper in his high garret, and whipping his flagging brain with fierce stimulant, while the printer's boy sits on the doorstep.

It stands alone. There is no book in the literature of the world quite like it. It is the challenge of youth and beauty to the world; and if we—grown wise and weary in the struggle—find a note of ferocity and extravagance in the challenge, then let us judge with understanding, and remember that it is a case of the fine and the weak against the brutal and the ignorant. Murger's voice is the voice of protesting youth. He is illogical; so is youth. He is furious; so is youth. He is heroic; so is youth. He is half-mad with indignation and half-mad with the joy of living; so is youth. It is by its very waywardness and disregard of values that the book captures us.

There is no other book in which the spirit of Paris breathes more easily. Here we have the essential Paris, just as in Thomas Dekker we have the essential London. Poets, novelists and essayists have set themselves again and again to ensnare the elusive Paris between the covers of a book; but Murger alone—though he writes of Paris in 1830—has succeeded. Those who have never been to Paris should first read his book; then, when they do go, they will experience the sense of coming back to some known place.

It was this insidious book that first tempted

youth to escape from a hidebound world; showed it the way out—a way beset by delightful hazards. It offered to all the golden boys and girls a new Utopia, and they were fain to visit it. That it was a false world troubled them not at all. The green glass, the delirious midnight hours, and the pale loveliness of Mimi and Musette were, perhaps, shackles as binding and as fearful as those of Convention. But anything to escape from the irk and thrall of their narrow realities; so away they went, and the end of the story is written in the archives of the Morgue.

After seventy years, however, the middle way has been found. There are few tragedies to-day in the Quartier Latin, and very little gaiety or kindliness; none of the old adventurous spirit. Things are going too well in the studio-world these days. Chelsea and Montmartre have been invaded by the American dilettanti, whose lives are one long struggle to be Bohemians on a thousand a year. If, however, there be those who regard this state of things as an improvement on the old, then let it be remembered that this way was only found after Murger had wrecked his own life and the lives of those who followed so gaily the unkind path down which he led them. It is a pitiful catalogue; the more pitiful since so many of the young dead are anonymous—the young men who might, had they lived, have given the world so much of beauty, but who were unable to pull up short of the precipice. Some of them, of course, we know: Gerard de Nerval, Barbey d'Aurevilly, Baudelaire, Verlaine, Ernest Dowson; and their London monument is the Café Royal.

* * * * *

At half-past nine all fun ceased, but we had picked up a bunch from Fleet Street, one of whom was taking home two bottles of whisky. So we moved to "another place," and ordered black coffees which drank tolerably well—after some swift surreptitious business with a corkscrew. Later, we strolled across Oxford Street to what remained of the German Quarter. We visited various coffee-bars, where our genial comrade with the bottles again did his duty; did it beautifully, did it splendidly, did it with Vine Street at his ear. And in a grey street off Tottenham Court Road we found a poor man's cabaret. In the back room of a coffee-bar an entertainment was proceeding. Two schonk boys, in straw hats, were at a piano, assisted by an anæmic girl and a real coal-black coon, who gave us the essential rag-times of the South. The place was packed with the finest collection of cosmopolitan toughs I had ever seen in one room. The air, physical and moral, was hardly breathable, and as the boys were spoiling for a row, one misinterpreted glance would have brought trouble—and lots of it. At different tables, voices were raised in altercation, when not in lusty song, and the general impression the place gave me was that it was a squalid, dirty model of the old Criterion Long Bar. All the meaner, more desperate citizens of the law-breaking world were gathered here; and, though we had broken a few by-laws ourselves that night, we were not anxious to be led into any more shattering of the Doraic tables. So at midnight we adjourned to "another place," and drank dry gingers until three o'clock in the morning. Then, to a Turkish Bath, and so to bed; not very merry, but as cheered in the spirit as the humble, useless citizen is allowed to be in a miserable, hole-and-corner way in wartime.

It had been a sorry experience, this round of visits, in 1917, to quarters last seen in 1914; and it made me curious to know how other familiar nooks had received the wanton assault of kings. In the haphazard sketches that follow I have tried to catch the external war-time atmosphere of a few of the old haunts, so far as a poor reporter may. Later, perhaps, a better hand than mine will discover for us the essential soul of London under siege; and these rough notes may be of some service, since all remembrance of that time was blown away from most minds by the maroons of Armistice Day.

BACK TO DOCKLAND

From my earliest perceiving moments, docks and railway stations have been, for me, the most romantic spots of the city in which I was born and bred. Quays and wharves, cuts, basins, reaches, steel tracks and passenger trains, and all that belonged to the life of the waterside and the railway, spoke to me of illimitable travel and distant, therefore desirable, things.

This feeling I share, I suppose, with millions of other men and children who have been reared in coast cities, and whose minds respond to the large invitations offered by sooty smoke-stacks or the dim outline of a station roof. And if these things pierced the complacence of one's days in the past, how much deeper and more significant their message in those four dreadful years, when men fared forth in ships and trains to new perils unimagined in the quieter years.

That apart, I see docks and railway stations not in their economic or historic aspect, but in the picturesque light, as, perhaps, the most emphatic glory of London. For London's major architectural beauties I care little. Abbeys, cathedrals, old churches, museums, leave me cold; the fine shudder about the shoulders I suffer most sharply before those haphazard wizardries of brick and iron flung together by the exigencies of modern commerce. Their fortuitous ugliness achieves a new beauty. A random eye-full of such townscapes may yield only an impression of squalor, but many acres of squalor produce, by their very vastness, something of the sublime. Belching chimneys, flaring furnaces, the solemn smell of wet coal mingled with that of tar and bilge-water, and the sight of brown sails and surly funnels and swinging cranes—in these misshapen masses I find that delight that others receive from contemplation of Salisbury Cathedral or a spire of Wren's.

The docks of London lie closely in a group—Wapping, Shadwell, Rotherhithe, Poplar, Limehouse, Isle of Dogs, Blackwall, and North Woolwich, and each possesses its own fine-flavoured character. You may know at once, without other evidence than that afforded by the sense of smell, whether you stand in London Docks, Surrey Commercial Docks, West India Docks, Millwall Docks, or Victoria and Albert Docks. To me, the West and East India Docks are soaked in the bright odour and placid clamour of the East, with something of feminine allure in the quality of their appeal. Victoria and Albert Docks I find gaunt and colourless. Surrey Commercial Docks remind me of some coarse merchant from the Royal Exchange, stupidly vulgar in speech, clothes and character.

The East and West India Docks I have treated elsewhere. Of the others, the most exciting are Millwall and London Docks—though of the latter I fear one must now speak in the past tense. Shadwell High Street and St. George's, which border the London Docks, are no longer themselves. All is now charged with gloom, broken only by the anæmic lights of a few miserable mission-halls and coffee-bars for the use of Scandinavian seamen. Awhile back, before this monstrous jest of war, there was a certain raw gaiety about the place brought thither by these same blond vikings; but, since the frenetic agitations of certain timorous people against "all aliens"—as though none but an alien can be a spy—these men are not now allowed to land from their boats, and Shadwell is the poorer of a touch of colour. One might often meet them and fraternize with them in the coffee-bars and beer-shops (there are few "public-houses" in these streets), and hear their view of things. Bearded giants they were, absurdly out of the picture in these tiny, sawdusted rooms, against the hideous bedizenment of the London house of refreshment. They would engage in rich, confused, interminable conversations, using a language which, to the stranger, sounded like a medley of hiccoughs and snorts; and there would be vehement arguments and a large fanning of the breeze. In the upper rooms, on Saturday evenings, one might have singing and dancing to a cracked piano and a superannuated banjo, and there the girls of the quarter would appear, and would do themselves well on seafarers' hospitality.

But the free-and-easy atmosphere is gone. You enter any bar and are at once under a cloud. Suspicion has been bred in all these docks men by the cheap Press. The patriotic stevedores re-- gard you as a disguised alien. The landlord wonders whether you are one of those blasted newspaper men or are from the Yard. The visitors to the bars are in every case insipid; none of the ripe character that once lit such places to sudden life. Abrupt acquaintance and casual conversation are not to be had. The beer is filthy. The good Burton is gone, and in its place you have a foul concoction which has not the mellowing effect of honest British beer or the exhilarating effect of the light continental brews. Shadwell High Street is now a dirty lane of poor lodging-houses, foul courts, waste tracts of land, mission halls exuding a stale air of diseased hospitality, and those nondescript establishments, ships' chandlers, with their miscellanies of apparently useless lumber, stored in such a heap that it would seem impossible to find any article immediately required. In short, social life here is as it should be, according to the unwearied in war-work.

Still, there are some adorable morsels of domestic architecture to be found up narrow alleys: old cottages and tumbling buildings, mellowed by centuries of association with many weathers and with men and ships from the green and golden seas that lie beyond the muddy waters of London River; and these supply one touch of animation to the prevailing moribundity.

Very different are the Millwall Docks. Little material beauty here, but something much better —good company, and plenty of it. The docks lie at the south of the Isle of Dogs, amid a flat stretch of dreary warehouses and factories, and you approach them by a long curving street of poor cottages and "general" shops. The island is a place of harsh discords, for Cubitt's works are established here, and the ring of hammers rises above the roar of furnaces, and the vociferous life of the canals above the scream of the siren and the moan of the hooter, and the concerted voices of the island seem to cry the accumulated agony of the East End. Great arc lights, suspended from above, when cargoes are being unloaded by night, fling into sudden illumination or shadow the faces and figures of the groups of workers as they stagger up the gangways with their loads, and lend to the whole scene an air of theatrical illusion. In the bars you find sweaty engineers and grimy stokers. Here is a prolific field of character; mostly British, though a few Lascars may be found, drinking solitary drinks or parading the streets with their customary air of bewilderment. Here are nut-brown toilers of the sea, whose complexions suggest that they have been trapped by that advertiser in the popular Press who offers his toilet wares with the oracular pronouncement that "Handsome Men

Are Slightly Sunburnt." Here are men who have circled the seven seas. Here, calm and taciturn, is a man who knows Pitcairn Islanders to speak to; who produces from one pocket a carved ivory god, presented to him by some native of Java, and from the other Old Timothy's One-Horse Snip for the Big Race.

Under the meagre daylight and the opulent shadows of these docks you may drink beer and listen to casual chit-chat that carries you round the world and into magical hidden places, and brings you back with a jerk to the Isle of Dogs.

"Yerce. Two bob a pound the 'Ome an' Colonial was arstin' the missus for the stuff. I soon went round an' told 'em where they could put it. Well, 'sI was sayin', after we left Rangoon, we——"

The land in this district consists, for the most part, of oozing marsh, so that, when a gale sweeps from the mouth of the river, it reaches the island with unexpended force. Then the sky seems to scream in harmony with the rattling windows. Saloon signs swing grotesquely. The river assumes a steely hue, heaving and rushing, sucking against staples, wharves and barges, and rising in ineffectual splashes against the gates of the docks, until you seek the public bar of the " Dog and Thunderstorm " as a sanctuary. There, amid the babble of pewter and glass and the punctuation of the cash register, you forget any London gale in listening to stories of typhoons, cyclones, and other freaks of the elements common to the Pacific and the meeting of the waters round the Horn.

Many hours have I squandered on the ridiculous bridge of the Isle of Dogs, in sunlight or twilight, grey mist or velvet darkness, building my dreams about the boats as they dropped downstream to the oceans of the world and their ports with honey-syllabled names—Swatow, Rangoon, Manila, Mozambique, Amoy—returning in normal times, with fantastic cargoes of cornelian and jade, malachite and onyx, fine shapes of ivory and coral, sharp spices of betel-nut and bhang, and a secret tin or two of li-un—perhaps not returning at all. There I would stand, giving to each ship some name and destination born of my own fancy, and endowing it with a marvellous meed of adventure.

It is an exciting experience for the landsman Cockney, strolling the streets about the docks, to rub shoulders with other little Cockneys, in blue serge and cotton scarves, who have accepted the non-committal invitation offered by the funnel and the rigging over the walls of Limehouse Basin. One remembers the story of the pale curate at the church concert, at which one of the entertainers had sung a setting of Kipling's "Rolling Down to Rio." "Ah, God!" he said, wringing his thin hands, "that's what I often feel like. . . . Rolling down to Rio." And in these streets one meets insignificant little men who have done it; who have rolled down to Rio and gone back to Mandalay, and seen the dawn come up like thunder outer China 'crost the Bay

And I am proud to have nodding acquaintance with them. I am glad they have drunk beer with me. I am glad I have clicked the chopsticks in Limehouse Causeway with the yellow boys who can talk of Canton and Siam and North Borneo and San Francisco. I am glad I have salaamed noble men of India at the Asiatics' Home, and heard their stories of odourous villages in the hills and of the seas about India, and of strange islands which mere Cockneys pick out on the map with an uncertain forefinger—Andamans, Nicobars, Solomons, and so forth. I am glad from having met men who know Java as I know London; who know the best places in Tokio for tea and the most picturesque spots in Formosa; who can direct me to a good hotel in Singapore, should I ever go there, and who know where Irish whisky can be bought in Sarawak. Why study guide-books, or consult with the omniscient Mr. Cook, when you may find about the great ornamental gates of the docks of London natives of all corners of the world who can provide you with a hundred exclusive tips which will make smooth the traveller's way over every obstacle or untoward incident? Indeed, why travel at all, when you may travel by proxy; when, by hanging round the docks of London, you may travel, on the lips of these men, through jungle, ocean, white town, palm grove, desert island, and suffer all the sharp sensations of standing silent upon a peak in Darien, the while you are taking heartening draughts of mild and bitter in the saloon bar of the " Star of the East "?

CHINATOWN REVISITED

"CHINATOWN, my Chinatown, where the lights are low"—a fragment of a music-hall song in praise of Chinatown which sticks ironically in my memory. The fact that the lights are low applies at the time of writing to the whole of London; and as for the word "Chinatown," which once carried a perfume of delight, it is now empty of meaning save as indicating a district of London where Chinamen live. To-day Limehouse is without salt or savour; flat and unprofitable; and of all that it once held of colour and mystery and the macabre, one must write in the past tense. The missionaries and the Defence of the Realm Act have together stripped it of all that furtive adventure that formerly held such lure for the Westerner.

It was in 1917 that I returned to it, after an absence of some years. In that year I received an invitation that is rightly accepted as a compliment: I was asked by Alvin Langdon Coburn to meet him at his studio, and let him make from my face one of those ecstatic muddles of grey and brown that have won for him the world's acknowledgment as the first artist of the camera. Our meeting discovered a mutual enthusiasm for Limehouse, and we arranged an excursion. There, we said to ourselves, we shall find yet a taste of the pleasant things that the world has forgotten: soft movement, solitude, little courtesies, as well as wonderful things to buy. There we shall find sharp-flavoured things to eat and drink, and josses and chaste carvings, and sharp knives. Oh, and the tea, too—the little two-ounce packets of suey-sen at sevenpence, that clothe the hour of five o'clock with delicate scents and dreams.

But the suey-sen was gone, done to death by the tea-rationing order. Gone, too, was the bland iniquity of the place. Our saunter through Pennyfields and the Causeway was a succession of disillusions. The spirit of the commercial and controlled West breathed on us from every side. All the dusky delicacies were suppressed. Dora had stepped in and khyboshed the little haunts that once invited to curious amusement. Opium, li-un, and other essences of the white poppy, secretly hoarded, were fetching £30 per pound.

The hop-hoads had got it in the neck, and the odour of gin-seng floated seldom upon the air. The old tong feuds had been suppressed by stern policing, and Thames Police Court had become almost as suave and seemly as Rumpelmayer's. Even that joyous festival, the Feast of the Lanterns, kept at the Chinese New Year, had fallen out of the calendar. The Asiatic seamen had been made good by an Order in Council. All for the best, no doubt; yet how one missed the bizarre flame and salt of the old Quarter.

We found Pennyfields and the Causeway uncomfortably crowded, for the outward mail sailings were reduced, and the men who landed in the early days had been unable to get away. So the streets and lodging-houses were thronged with Arabs, Malays, Hindoos, South Sea Islanders, and East Africans; and the Asiatics' Home for Destitute Orientals was having the time of its life. Every cubicle in the hotel was engaged, and many wanderers were sleeping where they could. Those with money paid for their accommodation; for the others, a small grant from the India Office secured them board and bed until such time as proper arrangements could be made. The kitchens were working overtime, for each race or creed has its own inexorable laws in the matter of food. Some eat this and some eat that, and others will eat anything—save pork—provided that prayers are spoken over it by an appointed priest.

At half-past nine an occasional tipsy Malay might be seen about the streets, but the old riots and mêlées were things of the past. In the little public-house at the corner of Pennyfields we found the usual crowd of Chinks and white girls, and the electric piano was gurgling its old sorry melodies, and beer and whisky were flowing; but the whole thing was very decorous and war-timish.

We did, however, find one splash of colour. A new and very gaudy restaurant had lately been opened in a narrow by-street, and here we took a meal of noodle, chow-chow and awabi, and some tea that was a mocking echo of the old suey-sen. The room was crowded with yellow boys and a few white girls. Suddenly, from a corner table, occupied by two of the ladies, came a sharp stir. A few heated words rattled on the air, and then one rose, caught the other a resounding biff in the neck, and screamed at her:—

"You dare say I'm not respectable! I *am* respectable. I come from Manchester."

This evidence the assaulted one refused to regard as final. She rose, reached over the table, and clawed madly at her opponent's face and clothes. Then they broke from the table, and fought, and fell, and screamed, and delivered the hideous animal noises made by those who see red. At once the place boiled. I've never been in a Chinese rebellion, but if the clamour and the antics of the twenty or so yellow boys in that café be taken as a faint record of such an affair, it is a good thing for the sensitive to be out of. To the corner dashed waiters and some customers, and there they rolled one another to the floor in their efforts to separate the girls, while others stood about and screamed advice in the various dialects of the Celestial Empire. At last the girls were torn apart, and struggled insanely in half a dozen grips as they hurled inspired thoughts at one another, or returned to the old chorus of " Dirty prostitute." " I ain't a prostitute. I come from Manchester. Lemme gettater."

And with a final wrench the respectable one did get at her. She broke away, turned to a table, and with three swift gestures flung cup, saucer and sauce-boat into the face of her traducer. That finished it. The proprietor had stood aloof while the girls tore each other's faces and bit at uncovered breasts. But the sight of his broken crockery acted as a remover of gravity. He dashed down the steps, pushed aside assistants and advisers, grabbed the nearest girl—the respectable one—round the waist, wrestled her to the top of the marble stairs that lead from the door to the upper restaurant, and then, with a sharp knee-kick, sent her headlong to the bottom, where she lay quiet.

Whereupon her opponent crashed across a table in hysterics, kicking, moaning, laughing and sobbing: " You've killed 'er—yeh beast. You've killed 'er. She's my pal. Oo. Oo. Oooooowh!"

This lasted about a minute. Then, suddenly, she arose, pulled herself together, ran madly down the stairs, picked up her pal, and staggered with her to the street. At once, without a word of comment, the company returned placidly to its eating and drinking; and this affair—an event in the otherwise dull life of Limehouse—was over.

Years ago, such affairs were of daily occurrence, and the West India Dock Road became a legend to frighten children with at night. But the times change. Chinatown is a back number, and there now remains no corner to which one may take the curious visitor thirsting for exotic excitement—unless it be the wilds of Tottenham. The Chinatown of New York, too, has become respectable. The founder of that colony, Old Nick, died recently, in miserable circumstances, after having acquired thousands of dollars by his enterprise. From the high estate of Founder of the Chinatown he dropped to the position of panhandler, swinging on the ears of his compatriots. About forty years ago, when Mott Street, Pell Street, and Doyers Street were the territory of the Whyos, the Bowery boys and the Dead Rabbits, Old Nick crept stealthily into a small corner. He started a cigar-store in Mott Street, making his own cigars. He was honest, thrifty, and possessed a lust for work. The cigar-store prospered, and soon, feeling lonely, as the only Chink among so many white boys, he passed the word to his countrymen about the big spenders of the district. On his advice, they closed their laundries and came to live alongside, to get their pickings from the dollars that were flying about. Chinatown was started, and rapidly developed, and its atmosphere was sedulously " arranged " for the benefit of conducted tourists from uptown, and the tables rattled with the dice and fluttered with the cards. This success was the beginning of Old Nick's failure. At the tables he lost all: his capital, his store, his home, and his proud position. For a time he managed to survive in fair circumstances; but soon the hatchet men became too numerous, and their tong feuds too deadly, and their gambling tricks too notorious. Police raids and the firm hand of the higher Chinese merchants put a stop to the prosperity of Chinatown, and soon it fell away to nothing, and Old Nick passed his last days on the sporadic charity of a white woman whom he had in happier days befriended.

And to-day Pell Street and Mott Street are as quiet and virtuous as Pennyfields and the Causeway. Coburn and I left the old waterside streets with feelings of dismay, tasting ashes in the mouth. We tried to draw from an old storekeeper, a topside good-fella chap, some expression of his own attitude to present conditions, but with his usual impassivity he passed it over. How could this utterly debased and miserable one who dares to stand before noble and refined ones from Office of Printed Leaves, who have honoured his totally inadequate establishment with symmetrical presences, presume to offer to exalted intelligences utterly insignificant thoughts that find lodging in despicable breast?

Clearly he was handing us the lemon, so we took it, and departed for the more reckless joys of Hammersmith, where Coburn has his home. On the journey back I remembered the drabness we had just left, and then I remembered Limehouse as it was—a pool of Eastern filth and metropolitan squalor; a place where unhappy Lascars, discharged from ships they were only too glad to leave, were at once the prey of rascally lodging-house keepers, mostly English, who fleeced them over the fan-tan tables and then slung them to the dark alleys of the docks. A wicked place; yes, but colourful.

Listen to the following: two extracts from an East End paper of thirty years back:—

THAMES POLICE COURT.

John Lyons, who keeps a common lodging-house, which he has neglected to register, appeared before Mr. Ingram in answer to a summons taken out by Inspector Price. J. Kirby, 53A, inspector of common lodging-houses, stated that on Saturday night last he visited defendant's house, which was in a most filthy and dilapidated condition. In the first floor he found a Chinaman sleeping in a cupboard or small closet, filled with cobwebs. The wretched creature was without a shirt, and

CHINATOWN REVISITED

was covered with a few rags. The Chinaman was apparently in a dying state, and has since expired. An inquest was held on his remains, and it was proved he died of fever, and had been most grossly neglected. The room in which the Chinaman lay was without bedding or furniture. In the second room he found Aby Callighan, an Irishwoman, who said she paid 1s. 6d. a week rent. In the third room was Abdallah, a Lascar, who said he paid 3s. per week, and a Chinaman squatting on a chair smoking. In the fourth room was Dong Yoke, a Chinaman, who said he paid 2s. 6d. per week for the privilege of sleeping on the bare boards; two Lascars on bedsteads smoking opium, and the dead body of a Lascar lying on the floor, and covered with an old rug. In the fifth room was an Asiatic seaman, named Peru, who said he paid 3s. per week, and eleven other Lascars, six of whom were sleeping on bedsteads, three on the floor, and two on chairs. If the house were registered, only four persons would be allowed in the room. The effluvium, caused by smoking opium and the over-crowded state of the room, was most nauseous and intolerable. In the kitchen, which was very damp, he found Sedgoo, who said he had to pay 2s. a week, and eight Chinamen huddled together. The stench here was very bad. If the house were registered, no one would have been allowed to inhabit the kitchen at all. He should say the house was quite unfit for a human habitation. The floors of the rooms, the stairs and passages were in a filthy and dilapidated condition, covered with slime, dirt, and all kinds of odious substances.

The men had been hung up with weights tied to their feet; flogged with a rope; pork, the horror of the Mohammedan, served out to them to eat, and the insult carried further by violently ramming the tail of a pig into their mouths and twisting the entrails of the pig round their necks; they were forced up aloft at the point of the bayonet, and a shirt all gory with Lascar blood was exhibited on the trial, and all this proved in evidence. One man leaped overboard to escape his tormentor; a boat was about to be lowered to save the drowning man, but it was prohibited, and he was left to perish. The captain escaped out of the country, forfeiting his bail and abandoning his ship, leaving his chief officer to be brought to trial and to undergo punishment for his share of this cruel transaction.

In those days you might stand in West India Dock Road, on a June evening, in a dusk of blue and silver, the air heavy with the reek of betel nut, chandu and fried fish; the cottages stewing themselves in their viscid heat. Against the skyline rose Limehouse Church, one of the architectural beauties of London. Yellow men and brown ambled about you, and a melancholy guitar tinkled a melody of lost years. Then, were colour and movement; the whisper of slippered feet; the adventurous uncertainty of shadow; heavy mist, which never lifts from Poplar and Limehouse; strange voices creeping from nowhere; and occasionally the rasp of a gramophone delivering records of interminable Chinese dramas. The soul of the Orient wove its spell about you, until, into this evanescent atmosphere, came a Salvation Army chorus bawling a lot of emphatic stuff about glory and blood, or an organ with "It ain't all lavender!" and at once the clamour and reek of the place caught you.

Thirty years ago—that was its time of roses. Then, indeed, things did happen: things so strong that the perfume of them lingers to this day, and

CHINATOWN REVISITED

one can, remembering them, sometimes sympathize with those who say "LIMEHOUSE" in tones of terror. One of my earliest memories is of the West India Dock Road on a wet November afternoon. A fight was on between a Chink and a Malay. The Chink used a knife in an upward direction, forcefully. The Malay got the Chink down, and jumped with heavy boots on the bleeding yellow face.

Some time ago, when my ways were cast in that district, the boys would loaf at a kind of semi-private music-hall, attached to a public-house, where one of the Westernized Chinks, a San Sam Phung, led the band, and freely admitted all friends who bought him drinks. Every night he climbed to his chair, and his yellow face rose like a November sun over the orchestra-rail. When the conductor's tap turned on the flow of the dozen instruments, which blared rag-tag music, we shifted to the babbling bar and tried to be amused by the show. It was the dustiest thing in entertainment that you can imagine. To this day the hall stinks of snarling song. Dusty jokes we had, dusty music, dusty dresses, dusty girls to wear them, or take them off; and only the flogging of cheap whisky to carry us through the evening.

Solemn smokes of cut plug and indifferent cigar swirled in a haze of lilac, and over the opiate air San's fiddle would wail, surging up to the balcony's rim and the cloud of corpse faces that swam above it. More and more mephitic the air would grow, and noisier would become voice and foot and glass; until, with a burst of lights, and the roar of the chord-off from the band, the end would come, and we would tumble out into the great road where were the winking river, and keen air and sanity.

Later, the boys would shuffle along with San Sam Phung to his lodging over a waterside wine-shop, crossing the crazy bridge into the Isle of Dogs. Often, passing at midnight, you might have heard his heart-song trickling from an open window. He cared only for the modern, Italianate stuff, and would play it for hours at a time. Seated in the orchestra, in his second-hand dress-suit and well-oiled hair, he looked about as picturesque as a Bayswater boarding-house. But you should have seen him afterwards, during the day, in his one-room establishment, radiant in spangled dressing-gown and tempestuous hair, a cigarette at his lips, his fiddle at his chin. It was worth sitting up late for. Then his face would shine, if ever a Chink's can, and his bow would tear the soul from the fiddle in a fury of lyricism.

Half his room was filled with a stove, which thrust a long neck of piping ten feet in the wrong direction, and then swerved impulsively to the window. In the corner was a joss. The rest of the room was littered with fiddles and music. Over the stove hung a gaudy view of Amoy. He never tired of talking of Amoy, his home. He longed to get back to it—to flowers, blue waters, white towns. He lived only for the moment when he might tuck his fiddle-case under his arm and return to Amoy, home and beauty. Once started on the tawdry ribaldry which he had to play at the hall, his arm and fingers following mechanically the sheet before him, he would set his fancies free, and, like a flock of rose-winged birds, they took flight to Amoy. Music, for him, was just melody —the graceful surface of things; in a word Amoy. Often he confessed to a terrible fear that he would grow old and die among our swart streets ere he could save enough to return. And he did. Full of the poppy one dark night, he stepped over the edge of a wharf at Millwall. Then, at the inquiry, it was discovered that his nostalgia for Amoy was pure fake. He had never been there.

He was born on a boat that crawled up-river one foggy morning, and had never for a day gone out of London.

There were many other delightful creatures of Limehouse whose names lie persistently on the memory. There was Afong, a chimpanzee who ran a pen-yen joint. There was Chinese Emma, in whose establishment one could go "sleigh-riding." There was Shaik Boxhoo, a gentleman who did unpleasant things, and finally got religion and other advantages over his less wily brothers, who got only the jug. Faults they had in plenty, these throwbacks, but their faults were original. Every one of them was a bit of sharp-flavoured character, individual and distinct.

In those days there was a waste patch of wan grass, called The Gardens, near the Quarter, and something like a band performed there once a week. O Carnival, Carnival! There the local crowd would go, and there, to the music of dear Verdi, light feet would clatter about the asphalt walk, and there would happen what happens every Sunday night in those parts of London where are parks, promenades, bandstands and monkeys' parades. In the hot spangled dusk, the groups of girls, brave with best frocks and daring ribbons, would fling their love and their laughter to all who would have them. Through the plaintive music—poor Verdi! how like a wheezy music-box his crinoline melodies sounded, even then!—would swim little ripples of laughter when the girls were caressing or being caressed; and always the lisp of feet and the whisk of darling frocks kissing little black shoes.

Near by was the old "Royal Sovereign," which had a skittle-alley. There would gather the lousy Lascars, and there they would roll, bowl or pitch. Then they would swill. Later, they would roll, bowl or pitch, with a skinful of gin, through the reeling streets to whichever boat might claim them.

The black Lascars, unlike their yellow mates, are mostly disagreeable people. There was, in those days, but one of them who even approached affability. He was something of a Limehouse Wonder, for, in a sudden fight over spilt beer, he showed amazing aptitude not only with his fists, but also in ringcraft. Chuck Lightfoot, a local sport, happened to see him, and took him in hand, and for some years he stayed in Shadwell, putting one after another of the local lads to sleep. He finished his ring career in a dockside saloon by knocking out an offending white man who had chipped him about his colour. It was a foul blow, and the man died. Pennyfields Polly got twelve months, and when he came out he started on the poppy and the snow, for he was not allowed to fight again, and life held nothing else for him. His friends tried to dissuade him, on the ground that he was ruining his health—a sensible argument to put to a man who had no interest in life; they might as well have told an Arctic explorer, who had lost the trail, that his tie was creeping up the back of his neck.

It is curious how the boys cling to you after a brief interchange of hospitalities. You drop into a beer-shack one evening, and you are sure to find a friend. One makes so easily in these parts a connection, salutations, fugitive intimacy. You are suddenly saluted, it may be by that good old friend, Mr. Lo, the poor Indian, or John Sam Ling Lee. Vaguely you recall the name. Yes; you stood him a drink, some ten years ago. Where has he been? Oh, he found a boat . . . went round the Horn . . . stranded at Lima . . . been in Cuba some time . . . got to Swatow later . . . might stay in London . . . might get a boat on Saturday.

But these casual encounters are now hardly

to be had. So many boys, so many places have disappeared. Blue Gate Fields, scene of many an Asiatic demonism, is gone. The " Royal Sovereign "—the *old* " Royal Sovereign "—is gone, and the Home for Asiatics reigns in its stead. The hop-shacks about the Poplar arches and the closed courtyards and their one-story cottages are no more. To-day—as I have said three times already; stop me if I say it again—the glamorous shame of Chinatown has departed. Nothing remains save tradition, which now and then is fanned into life by such a case as that of the drugged actress. Yet you may still find people who journey fearfully to Limehouse, and spend money in its shops and restaurants, and suffer their self-manufactured excitements while sojourning in its somnolent streets among the respectable sons of Canton. The boys will not thank me for robbing them of the soft marks who pay twenty shillings for a jade bangle, of the kind sold in a sixpenny-halfpenny bazaar; so, anticipating their celestial disapproval, this miserable prostrates himself and remains bowed for their gracious pardon, and begs to be permitted to say that the entirely inadequate benedictions of this one will be upon them until the waning of the last moon.

SOHO CARRIES ON

Soho! Soho!

Joyous syllables, in early times expressive of the delights of the chase, and even to-day carrying an echo of nights of festivity, though an echo only. How many thousand of provincials, seeing London, have been drawn to those odourous byways that thrust themselves so briskly through the staid pleasure-land of the West End—Greek Street, Frith Street, Dean Street, Old Compton Street: a series of interjections breaking a dull paragraph—where they might catch the true Latin temper and bear away to the smoking-rooms of country Conservative clubs fulsome tales that have made Soho already a legend. Indeed, I know one cautious lad from Yorkshire, whose creed is that You Never Know and You Can't Be Too Careful, who always furnishes himself with a loaded revolver when dining with a town friend in Soho. I am not one to look sourly upon the simple pleasures of the poor; I do not begrudge him his concocted dish of thrills. I only mention this trick of his because it proves again the strange resurrective powers of an oft-buried lie. You may sweep, you may garnish Soho if you will; but the scent of adventure will hang round it still. But to-day the scent is very faint. The streets that once rang with laughter and prodigal talk are in A.D. 1917 charged with gloom; their gentle noise is pitched in the minor key. These morsels of the South, shovelled into the swart melancholies of central London, have lost their happy summer tone. Charing Cross Road was always a streak of misery, but, on the most leaden day, its side streets gave an impression of light. Lord knows whence came the light. Not from the skies. Perhaps from the indolently vivacious loungers; perhaps from the flower-boxes on the window-sills, or the variegated shops bowered with pendant polonies, in rainbow wrappings of tinfoil, and flasks of Chianti. One always walked down Old Compton Street with a lilt, as to some carnival tune. Nothing mattered. There were macaroni and spaghetti to eat, and Chianti to drink; dishes of ravioli; cigars at a halfpenny a time and cigarettes at six a penny; copies of frivolous comic-papers; and delicate glasses of lire, a liqueur that carried you at the first sip to the green-hued Mediterranean. The very smell of the place was the smell of those lovable little towns of the Midi. But all is now changed. Gone are the shilling tables-d'hôte and their ravishing dishes. Gone is the pint of vin ordinaire at tenpence. Will they ever come again, those gigantic, lamp-lit evenings, those Homeric bob's-worths of hors-d'œuvre, soup, omelette, chicken, cheese and coffee? Shall we ever again cross Oxford Street to the old German Quarter and drink their excellent Pilsener and Munchner, in heartening steins, and eat their leber-wurst sandwiches, and smoke their long, thin cigars? Or seat ourselves in the Schweitzerhof, where four wonderful dishes were placed before you at a cost of tenpence by some dastard spy, in the pay of that invisible-cloak artist, the English Bolo?—who doubtless reported to Berlin our conversation about Phyllis Monkman's hair and Billy Merson's technique. Nay, I think not. The blight of civilization is upon Soho. Many once cosy and memorable cafés are closed. Other places have altered their note and become uncomfortably English; while those that retain their atmosphere and their customers have considerably changed their menu and cuisine. One-and-ninepence is the lowest charge for a table-d'hôte—and pretty poor hunting at that. The old elaborate half-crown dinners are now less elaborate and cost four shillings. And the wine-lists—well, wouldn't they knock poor Omar off his perch? I don't know who bought Omar's drinks, or whether he paid for his own, but if he lived in Soho to-day he'd have a pretty thin time either way—unless the factory price for tents had increased in proportion with other things.

Gone, too, is the delicious atmosphere of *laisser-faire* that made Soho a refreshment of the soul for the visitors from Streatham and Ealing. Soho's patrons to-day have a furtive, guilty look about them. You see, they are trying to be happy in war-time. No more do you see in the cafés the cold-eyed anarchists and the petty bourgeois and artisans from the foreign warehouses of the locality. In their place are heavy-eyed women, placid and monosyllabic, and much khaki and horizon blue. Many of the British soldiers, officers and privates, are men who have not yet been out, and are experimenting with their French among the French girls who have taken the places of the swift-footed, gestic Luigi, François or Alphonse; others have come from France, where they have discovered the piquancy of French cooking, and desire no more the solidities of the " old English " chop-house.

Over all is an atmosphere of restraint. Gone are the furious argument and the preposterous accord. Gone are the colour and the loud lights and the evening noise. Soho is marking time, until the good days return—if ever. Not in 1917 do you see Old Compton Street as a line of warm and fragrant café-windows; instead, you stumble drunkenly through a dim, murky lane, and take your chance by pushing the first black door that exudes a smell of food. Gone, too, are those exotic foods that brought such zest to the jaded palate. The macaroni and spaghetti now being manufactured in London are poor substitutes for the real thing, being served in long, flat strips instead of in the graceful pipe form of other days. Camembert, Brie, Roquefort, Gruyère, Port Salut, Strachini and other enchanting cheeses are unobtainable; and you may cry in vain for edible snails and the savoury stew of frogs' legs. True, the Chinese café in Regent Street can furnish for the adventurous stomach such trifles as black eggs (guaranteed thirty years old), sharks' fins at seven shillings a portion, stewed seaweed, bamboo shoots, and sweet birds'-nests; but Regent Street is beyond the bounds of Soho.

Nevertheless, if you attend carefully, and if you are lucky, you may still catch in Old Compton Street a faint echo of its graces and picturesque melancholy. You may still see and hear the sombre Yid, the furious Italian, the yodelling Swiss, and the deprecating French, hanging about the dozen or so coffee-bars that have appeared since 1914. A few of these places existed in certain corners of London long before that date, but it is only lately that the Londoner has discovered them and called for more. The Londoner—I offer this fact to all students of national traits—must always lean when taking his refreshment. Certain gay and festive gentlemen, who constitute an instrument of order called the Central Control Board, forbid him to lean in those places where, of old, he was accustomed to lean; at any rate, he is only allowed to lean during certain defined hours. You might think that he would have gladly availed himself of this opportunity for resting awhile by sitting at a marble-topped table and drinking coffee or tea, or—horrid thought!—cocoa. But no; he isn't happy unless he leans over his refreshment; and the café-bar has supplied his demands. There is something in leaning against a bar which entirely changes one's outlook. You may sit at a table and drink whisky-and-soda, and yet not achieve a tithe of the expansiveness that is yours when you are leaning against a bar and drinking dispiriting stuff like coffee or sirop. Maybe the physical attitude reacts on the mind, and tightens up certain cords or sinews, or eases the blood-pressure; anyway, fears, doubts, and cautions seem to vanish in these little corners of France, and momentarily the old animation of Soho returns.

In these places you may perchance yet capture for a fleeting space the will-o'-the-wisperie of other days: movement and festal colour; laughter and quick tears; the warm jest and the darkling mystery that epitomize the city of all cities; and the wanton, rose-winged graces that flutter about the fair head of M'selle Lolotte, as she hands you your café nature and an April smile for sweetening, carry to you a breath of the glitter and spaciousness of old time. You do not know Lolotte, perhaps! Thousand commiserations, M'sieu! What damage! Is Lolotte lovely and delicate? But of a loveliness of the most ravishing! The shining hair and the eyes of the most disturbing!

Lolotte is in direct descent from Mimi Pinson, half angel and half puss.

Soldiers of all the Allied armies gather about her crescent-shaped bar after half-past nine of an evening. The floor is sawdusted. The counter is sloppy with overflows of coffee. Lips and nose receive from the air that bitter tang derived only from the smoke of Maryland tobacco. The varied uniforms of the patrons make a harmony of debonair gaiety with the many-coloured bottles of cordials and sirops.

"*Pardon, m'sieu!*" cries the poilu, as he accidentally jogs the arm by which Sergeant Michael Cassidy is raising his coffee-cup.

"*Oh, sarner fairy hang, mossoo! Moselle, donnay mwaw urn Granny Dean.*"

"*M'sieu parle français, alors?*"

"*Ah, oui. Jer parle urn purr.*"

And another supporting column is added to the structure of the Entente.

Over in the corner stands a little fat fellow. That corner belongs to him by right of three years' occupation. He is 'Ockington from a near-by printing works. Ask 'Ockington what he thinks about these 'ere coffee-bars.

"Ah," he'll say, "I like these Frenchified caffies. Grand idea, if you ask me. Makes yeh feel as though you was abroad-like. Gives yeh that Lazy-Fare feelin'. I bin abroad, y'know. Dessay you 'ave, too, shouldn't wonder. I don't blame yeh. See what yeh can while yeh can, 'ats what I say. My young Sid went over to Paris one Bang Koliday, 'fore the war, an' he come back as different again. Yerce, I'm all fer the French caffies, I am. Nicely got up, I think. Good meoggerny counter; and this floor and the walls—all done in that what-d'ye call it—mosey-ac. What I alwis say is this: the French is a gay nation. Gay. And you feel it 'ere, doncher? Sort of cheers you up, like, if yer know what I mean, to drop in 'ere for a minute or two. . . . Year or two ago, now, after a rush job at the Works, I used to stop at a coffee-stall on me way 'ome late at night, an' 'ave a penny cup o' swipes—yerce, an' glad *of* it. But the difference in the stuff they give yer 'ere—don't it drink lovely and smooth?"

Then his monologue is interrupted by the electric piano, which some one has fed with pennies; and your ear is charmed or tortured by the latest revue music or old favourites from Paris and Naples—" Marguerite," " Sous les ponts de

Paris," "Monaco," the Tripoli March. If you appear interested in the piano, whose voice Lolotte loves, she will offer to toss you for the next penn'orth. Never does she lose. She wins by the simple trick of snatching your penny away the moment you lift your hand from it, and gurgling delightedly at your discomfiture.

No wonder the coffee-bar has become such a feature of London life in this time of war. Leaning, in Lolotte's bar, is a real and not a forced pleasure. In the old days one could lean and absorb the drink of one's choice; but amid what company and with what service! Who could possibly desire to exchange fatigued inanities with the vacuous vulgarities who administer the ordinary London bar; who seem, like telephone girls, to have taken lessons from some insane teacher of elocution, with their "Nooh riarly?" expressive of incredulity; and their "Is yewers a Scartch, Mr. Iggulden?" But in Lolotte's bar, talk is bright, sometimes distinctly clever, and one lingers over one's coffee, chaffering with her for —well, ask 'Ockington how long he stays.

But Lolotte is not always gay. Sometimes she will tell you stories of Paris. There is a terrible story which she tells when she is feeling triste.

It is the story of a girl friend of hers with whom she worked in Paris. The girl grew ill; lost her work; and earned her living by the only possible means, until she grew too ill for that. One night Lolotte met her wearily walking the streets. She had been without food for two days, and had that morning been turned from her lodging. Suddenly, as they passed a florist's, she darted through its doors and inquired the price of some opulent blooms at the further end of the shop. The shopman turned towards them, and, as he turned, she dexterously snatched a bunch of white violets from a vase on the counter. The price of the orchids, she decided, was too high, and she came out.

Lolotte, who had seen the trick from the doorway, inquired the reason for the theft. And the answer was:

"Eh, bien; il faut avoir quelquechose quand on va rencontrer le bon Dieu."

Two days later her body, with a bunch of white violets fastened at the neck, was recovered from the Seine.

OUT OF TOWN

IT was an empty day, in the early part of the year, and I was its very idle singer; so idle that I was beginning to wonder whether there would be any Sunday dinner for me. I took stock of my possessions in coin, and found one-and-tenpence-halfpenny. Was I downhearted? Yes. But I didn't worry, for when things are at their worst, my habit is always to fold my hands and trust. Something always happens.

Something happened on this occasion: a double knock at the door and a telegram. It was from the most enlightened London publisher, whose firm has done so much in the way of encouraging young writers, and it asked me to call at once. I did so.

"Like to go to Monte Carlo?" he asked.

When I had recovered from the swoon, I begged him to ask another.

"Here's an American millionaire," he said,

"writing from Monte Carlo. He wants to write a book, and he wants some assistance. How would it suit you?"

I said it would suit me like a Savile Row outfit of clothes.

"When can you go?"

"Any old time."

"Right. You'd better wire him, and tell him I told you to. Don't let yourself go cheap. Good-bye."

I didn't fall on his neck in an outburst of gratitude: he wouldn't have liked it. But I yodelled and chirruped all the way to the nearest post-office, having touched a friend for ten shillings on the strength of the stunt. All that day and the next, telegrams passed between Monte Carlo and Balham. I asked a noble salary and expenses, and a wire came back: "Start at once." I replied: "No money." Ten pounds were delivered at my doorstep next morning, with the repeated message "Start at once."

But starting at once, in war-time, was not so easily done. There was a passport to get. That meant three days' lounging in a little wooden hut in the yard of the Foreign Office. Having got the passport, I spent four hours in a queue outside the French Consulate before I could get it *visé*. Six days after the first telegram, I stood shivering on Victoria Station at seven o'clock of a cadaverous January morning. Having been well and truly searched in another little hut, and having kissed the book, and sworn full-flavoured oaths about correspondence, and thought of a number, and added four to it, I was allowed to board the train.

Half the British Army was on that train, and Mr. Jerome K. Jerome and myself were the only civilians in our carriage. You will rightly guess that it was a lively journey. I had always wondered, in peace-time, why the jew's-harp was invented. I understand now. In the histories of this war, the jew's-harp will take as romantic a place as the pipes of Lucknow or the drums of Oude in the histories of other wars.

At Folkestone there were more searchings, more stamping of passports, more papers and "permissions" to bulk one's pocket and perplex one's mind. On the boat, standing-room only, and when a gestic stewardess sought seats for a fond mother and five little ones in the ladies' saloon, she found all places occupied by khaki figures stretched at full length.

"*Seulement les dames!*" she cried, pointing to a notice over the door.

"*Aha, madame!*" said a stalwart Australian, "*mais c'est la guerre!*" In other words "Aubrey Llewellyn Coventry Fell to you!"

Yes, it was war; and it was tactfully suggested to us by the crew, for, when we were clear of Folkestone harbour, all boats were slung out, and lifeboats were placed in tragic heaps on either side. It was a cold, angry sea, and stewards and stewardesses became aggressively prophetic about the fine crossing that we were to have. Germany had a few days before declared her first blockade of the English coast, and every speck on the sea became dreadfully portentous. At mid-Channel a destroyer stood in to us and ran up a stream of signals.

"This is it," chortled a Cockney, between violent trips to the side; "this is it! Now we're for it!"

Next moment I got a push in the back, and I thought it had come. But it was the elbow of one of the crew who had rushed forward, and was sorting bits of bunting from an impossibly tangled heap at my side. In about two seconds, he found what he wanted and hauled at a rope. Up went what looked like a patchwork counterpane, until the breeze caught it, when it became a string of shapes and colours, straining deliriously against its fastenings. Then down it came; then up again; then down; then up; then down; and that was the end of that conversation. I don't know what it signified, but half an hour later we were in Boulogne harbour.

More comic business with papers; then to the train. Yes, it was war. The bridge over the Oise had not then been repaired; so we crawled to Paris by an absurdly crab-like route. We left Boulogne just after twelve. We reached Paris at ten o'clock at night. There was no food on the train, and from six o'clock that morning, when I had had a swift cup of tea, until nearly midnight I got nothing in the way of refreshment. But who cared? I was going South to meet an American millionaire, and I had money in my pocket.

I arrived at Paris too late to connect with that night's P.L.M. express, so I had twenty-four hours to kill. I strolled idly about, and found Paris very little changed. There was an air about the people of irritation, of questioning, of petulant suffering; they had a manner expressive of "*A quoi bon?*" Somebody in high quarters had brought this thing upon them. Somebody in high quarters might rescue them from its evils—or might not. They moved like stricken animals, their habitual melancholy, which is often unnoticed because it is overlaid with vivacity, now permanently in possession.

I caught the night express to Monte Carlo. Our carriage contained eight sombre people, and the corridors were strewn with sleep-stupid soldiers. I was one sardine among many, and, with a twenty-seven-hour journey before me in this overheated, hermetically sealed sardine-tin, I began to think what a fool I had been to make this absurd journey to a place that was strange to me; to meet a millionaire about whom I knew nothing, and who might have changed his mind, millionaire-fashion, and left Monte Carlo by the time I got there; and to undertake a job which I might find, on examination, was beyond me.

Then, with a French girl's head on one shoulder, and my other twisted at an impossible angle into the window-frame, I went to sleep and awoke at Lyons, with a horrible headache and an unbearable mouth, the result of the boiling and over-spiced soup I had swallowed the night before. I think we all hated each other. It was impossible to wash or arrange oneself decently, and again there was no food on the train. But, as only the Latin mind can, we made the best of it and pretended that it was funny. Girls and men, complete strangers, drooped in abandonment against one another, or reclined on unknown necks. A young married couple behaved in a way that at other times would have meant a divorce. The husband rested his sagging head on the bosom of a stout matron, and a poilu stretched a rug across his knees and made a comfortable pillow for the little wife. *N'importe. C'était la guerre.*

On the platform at Lyons were groups of French Red Cross girls with wagons of coffee. This coffee was for the soldiers, but they handed it round impartially to civilians and soldiers alike, and those who cared could drop a few sous into the collecting basin. That coffee was the sweetest draught I had ever swallowed.

At Marseilles it was bright morning, and I was lucky enough to get a pannier, at a trifling cost of seven francs. These panniers are no meal for a hungry man. They contain a bone of chicken, a scrap of ham, a corner of Gruyère, a stick of bread (that surely was made by the firm that put the sand in sandwich), a half-bottle of sour white wine, a bottle of the eternal Vichy, Old Uncle Tom Cobleigh and all.

I had just finished it when we rolled into Toulon, and there I got my first glimpse of the true, warm South. I suffered a curious sense of " coming home." I had not known it, but all my childish dreams must have had for their background this coloured South, for, the moment it spread itself before me, bits of Verdi melodies ran through my heart and brain and I danced a double-shuffle. Since I was old enough to handle a fiddle, all music has interpreted itself to me in a visualization of blue seas, white coasts, green palms with lemon and nectarine dancing through them, and noisy, sun-bright towns, and swart faces and languorous and joyfully dirty people. The keenest sense of being at home came later, when, at Monte Carlo, I met Giacomo Puccini, the hero of my young days, whose music had illumined so many dark moments of my City slavery; who is in the direct line of succession from Verdi.

This first visit to Monte Carlo showed me Monte Carlo as she never was before. Half the hotels were closed or turned into hospitals, since all the German hotel-staffs had been packed home. In other times it would have been "the season," but now there was everywhere a sense of emptiness. Wounded British and French officers paraded the Terrace; disabled blacks from Algeria were on every hotel verandah or wandering aimlessly about the hilly streets with a sad air of being lost. The Casino was open, but it closed at eleven, and all the cafés closed with it; the former happy night-life had been nipped off short. At midnight the place was dead.

I was accommodated at an Italian *pension* in Beausoleil, which, in peace-times, was patronized by music-hall artists working the Beausoleil casino. The Casino had been turned into a barracks, but one or two Italian danseuses from the cabarets of San Remo were taking a brief rest, so that the days were less tiresome than they might have been. My millionaire was a charming man, who used my services but a few hours each day. Then I could dally with the sunshine and the Chianti and the breaking seas about the Condamine.

When I next want a cheap holiday I shan't go to Brighton, or Eastbourne, or Cromer; I shall go to Monte Carlo. The dear Italian Mama who kept the *pension* treated me like a prince for thirty-five francs a week. I had a large bedroom, with four windows looking to the Alpes Maritimes, and a huge, downy French bed; I had coffee and roll in the morning; a four-course lunch of Italian dishes, with a bottle of Chianti or Barolo; and a five-course dinner, again with a bottle. Those meals were the most delightful I have ever taken. The windows of the dining-room were flung wide to the Mediterranean, and between courses we could bask on the verandah while one of the girls would touch the guitar, the mandolin, or the accordion (sometimes we had all three going at once), in effervescent Neapolitan melody. My contribution to these meal-time entertainments was an English song of which they never tired: " The Man that Broke the Bank at Monte Carr-rr-lo! " Sometimes it was demanded five or six times in an evening. Immediately I arrived I was properly embraced and kissed by Mama and the three girls, and these rapturous kisses seemed to be part of the etiquette of the establishment, for they happened every morning and after all meals. M'selle Lola was allotted to me; a blonde Italian, afire with mischief and loving-kindness and little delicacies of affection.

On the third day of my visit I met a kindred

soul, the wireless operator from the Prince of Monaco's yacht, *L'Hirondelle,* which was lying in the harbour on loan to the French Government. He was a bright youth; had been many times on long cruises with the yacht, and spoke English which was as good as my French was bad. We had some delightful "noces" together, and it was in his company that I met and had talks with Caruso at the Café de Paris. An opera season was running at the Casino, and on opera nights the café remained open until a little past midnight. After the evening's work Caruso would drop into the café and talk with everybody. His naïve gratification when I told him how I had saved money for weeks, and had waited hours at the gallery door of Covent Garden to hear him sing, was delightful to witness. Prince George of Serbia was also there, recuperating; but though the Terrace at mid-day was crowded and pleasantly bright, I was told that against the Terrace in the old seasons it was miserably dull.

On ordinary nights, when we felt still fresh at eleven o'clock, we would take a car to Mentone, cross the frontier into Italy (which was not then at war), and spend a few cheery hours at Bordighera or San Remo, which were nightless. Then back to Monte Carlo at about five, to bed, and up again at nine, with no feeling of fatigue. It was curious to note how, under that sharp sunshine and keen night sky, all moral values were changed, or wholly obliterated. The first breath of the youthful company at the *pension* blew all London cobwebs away. It was all so abandoned, yet so sweet and wholesome; and, by contrast, the English seaside resort, where the girls play at " letting themselves go," was a crude and shameful farce. Whatever happened at Monaco seemed to be right; nothing was wrong except frigidity and unkindness.

My dear Italian Mama said to me one evening at dinner, when I had (in the English sense) disgraced myself by a remark straight from the heart:—

" *M'sieu Thomas, on m'a dit que les anglais ont froid. C'est pas vrai!* "

No, dear Mamina; but it was true before I stayed at the Pension Poggio at Beausoleil.

My work with the millionaire spread itself over two months; then, with a fat wad, I was free to return. It was not until I went to the Consulate to get my passport *visé* that I discovered how many war-time laws of France I had broken.

OUT OF TOWN

I had not registered myself on arrival; I had not reported myself periodically; and I had not obtained a *permis de séjour.* The Consul informed me cheerfully that heaps of trouble would be waiting for me when I went to the Mairie to get my *laissez-passer,* without which I could not buy a railway ticket. However, after being stood in a corner for two hours until all other travellers had received attention, a *laissez-passer* was thrown at me on my undertaking to leave Monte Carlo that night. A gendarme accompanied me to the station to see that I did so.

At Paris, a few hours spent with the police, the military, Hôtel-de-Ville, and the British Consulate resulted in permission to kick my heels there for a day or so.

A few mornings later arrived the millionaire's precious MS., which I had left behind so that he might revise it, with a message to hustle. I hustled. I reached London the same night. Next morning I negotiated with a publisher. In two days it was in the printer's hands and in a fortnight it was in the bookshops; and I was again out of a job.

IN SEARCH OF A SHOW

I HAVE been looking for a needle in a haystack, and I have not found it. I have been looking for an hour's true entertainment in London's theatres and music-halls during this spring season of 1918.

The tag of Mr. Gus Elen's old song, " 'E dunno where 'e are," very aptly describes the condition of the regular theatre-goer to-day. What would the old laddies of the Bodega-cheese days have thought, had any prophesied that at one swift step the Oxford and the Pavilion would simultaneously move into the ranks of the " legitimate;" that His Majesty's Theatre would be running a pantomime; that smoking would be allowed in the Lyceum, the Comedy, the Vaudeville, and the Garrick? Many people have lost their individuality by being merged into one or other war-movement since 1914; many streets have entirely lost those distinctive features which enable us to recognize them at one glance or by

IN SEARCH OF A SHOW

sound or smell; but nowhere has the war more completely smashed personality than in theatreland.

In the old days (one must use that pathetic phrase in speaking of ante-1914), the visitor to London knew precisely the type of entertainment and the type of audience he would find at any given establishment. To-day, one figures his bewilderment—verily, 'e dunno where 'e are. Formerly, he could be sure that at the Garrick he would find Mr. Bourchier playing a Bourchieresque part. At His Majesty's he would find just what he wanted—or would want what he found—for going to His Majesty's was not a matter of dropping in: it was a pious function. At the Alhambra or the Empire he would be sure of finding excellent ballet at about ten o'clock, when he could sip his drink, stroll round the promenade, and leave when he felt like it. At the time I write he finds Mr. Bourchier playing low comedy at a transformed music-hall, and at the Alhambra or the Empire he finds a suburban crowd, neatly seated in rows—father, mother and flappers—watching a quite innocuous entertainment.

Managers were long wont to classify in their

minds the "Garrick" audience, the "Daly" audience, the "Adelphi" audience, the "Haymarket" audience; and plays would be refused by a manager on the ground that "our audience wouldn't stand it; try the Lyric." To-day they are all in the melting-pot, and the poor habitué of the So-and-so Theatre has to take what is given him, and be mighty thankful for it.

At one time I loved a show, however cheap its kind; but in these days, after visiting a war-time show and suffering the feeling of assisting at some forbidden rite, I always wish I had wasted the evening in some other manner. Since 1914 the theatres have not produced one show that any sober man would pay two pence to see. The stuff that has been produced has paid its way because the bulk of the public is drunk—with war or overwork. The story of the stage since 1914 may be given in one word—"Punk." Knowing that we are all too preoccupied with solemn affairs to examine very closely our money's-worth, and knowing that the boys on leave are not likely to be too hypercritical, the theatrical money-lords —with one noble exception—have taken advantage of the situation to fub us off with any old store-room rubbish. We have dozens of genuine

IN SEARCH OF A SHOW 85

music-hall comedians on the stage to-day, but they are all slacking. Some of them get absorbed by West End shows, and at once, when they appear on the gigantic American stages of some of our modern theatres, surrounded by crowds of elephantine women, they lose whatever character and spontaneity they had. Others give the bulk of their time and brains to earning cheap notoriety by raising funds for charities or cultivating allotments—both commendable activities, but not compatible with the serious business of cheering the public. Gradually, the individual is being frozen out, and the stages are loaded with crowds of horsey, child-aping women, called by courtesy a beauty chorus; the show being called, also by courtesy, a revue. These shows resemble a revue as much as the short stories of popular magazines resemble a *conte*. They dazzle the eye and blast the ear, and, instead of entertaining, exhaust.

The artists have, allowing for human nature, done their best under trying circumstances; but playing to an audience of overseas khaki and tired working-people, who applaud their most maladroit japes, has had the effect of wearing them down. They no longer work. They take the easiest way, knowing that any remark about the

Kaiser, Old Bill, meat-cards, or the Better 'Ole is sure of a laugh.

One solitary example of money's-worth in wartime I found—but that is outside the lists of vaudeville or drama. I mean Sir Thomas Beecham's operative enterprise. Beginning, in 1915, to develop his previous tentative experiments—fighting against indifference, prejudice, often against active opposition—he went steadily on; and it is he whom our men must thank if, on returning, they find in England something besides factories and barracks. There is no man who, amid this welter of blood and hate, has performed work of higher national importance. While every effort was made to stifle or stultify every movement that made towards sanity and vision, he went doggedly forward, striving to save from the wreckage some trifle of sweetness and loveliness for those who have ears to hear. Had certain good people had their way, he, his ideals, his singers, his orchestra and his band instruments would have been flung into the general cesspool, to lie there and rot. But he won through; and I think only that enemy of civilization, the screaming, flag-wagging patriot, will disagree with a famous Major-General who, in full warpaint, stood at my side in the theatre bar between the acts of *Tristan,* and, turning upon a querulous civilian who had snorted against Wagner, cried angrily:—

"Nonsense, sir, nonsense. War is war. And music is music."

After years of struggling, Beecham has made it possible for an English singer to sing to English audiences under his English name, and has proved what theatrical and music-hall managers never attempt to prove: that England can produce her own native talent in music and drama, without taking the fourth-rate and fifth-rate, as well as the first-rate, material of America and the Continent. He has shown himself at once a philanthropist and a patriot. In none of his productions do we find signs of that cheap philosophy that "anything will do for war-time." Before the arrival of his company, opera in London was a mere social function which (except from the point of view of the galleryite) had little to do with music. People went to Covent Garden not to listen to music, but to be seen; just as they went to the Savoy or to the Carlton to be seen, not to procure nourishment. The Beecham opera is first and last a matter of music.

So, Sir Thomas, a few thousand of us take off our hats to you. I think we should all like to send you every morning a little bunch of violets, or something equally valueless, but symbolic of the fine things you have given us, of the silver lining you have disclosed to us in these over-clouded days.

VODKA AND VAGABONDS

Last year London lost two of its quaintest characters—Robertson, of Australia, that pathetic old man who haunted the Strand and carried in his hat a clumsily scrawled card announcing that he was searching for his errant daughter, and " Please Do Not Give Me Money "; and " Spring Onions," the Thames Police Court poet.

Now the race of London freaks seems ended. Craig, the poet of the Oval Cricket ground; Spiv Bagster; the Chiswick miser; Onions and Robertson; all are gone. Hunnable is confined; and G. N. Curzon isn't looking any too well. Even that prolific poet, Rowbotham, self-styled " the modern Homer," has been keeping quiet lately. It took a universal war, though, to make him nod.

I met " Spring " (privately, Mr. W. G. Waters) once or twice at Stepney. He was a vagrant minstrel of the long line of Villon and Cyrano de Bergerac. His anniversary odes were known to thousands of newspaper readers. He was the self-appointed Laureate of the nation.

He celebrated not only himself, his struggles and successes, but the pettier happenings of the day, such as the death of a king, the accession of a king, or the marriage of some royal couple. You remember his lines on the Coronation of Edward VII:—

The King, His Majesty, and may him Heaven bless,
He don't put no side on in his dress.
For, though he owns castles and palaces and houses,
He wears, just like you and me, coats and waistcoats and trousis.

The character of the genial Edward in four lines. Could it have been better said?

Not to know Spring argues yourself unknown. He might have stepped from the covers of Dekker's *Gull's Hornbook*. He was a child of nature. I can't bring myself to believe that he was born of woman. I believe the fairies must have left him under the gooseberry—no, under the laurel bush, for he wore the laurel, the myrtle, and the bay as one born to them. He also, on occasion, wore the vine-leaf; and surely that is now an honour as high as the laurel, since all good fellowship and kindliness and conviviality have been sponged from our social life. We have been made dull and hang-dog by law. I wonder what Spring would have said about that law in his unregenerate days—Spring, who was " in " thirty-nine times for " D. and D." He would have written a poem about it, I know: a poem that would have rung through the land, and have brought to camp the numerous army of Boltists, Thresholdists, and Snortists.

Oh, Spring has been one of the boys in his time, believe me. But in his latter years he was dull and virtuous; he kept the pledge of teetotalism for sixteen years, teetotalism meaning abstention from alcoholic liquors. This doesn't mean that he wasn't like all other teetotalers, sometimes drunk. The pious sages who make our by-laws seem to forget that it is as easy to get drunk on tea and coffee as on beer; the only difference being that beer makes you pleasantly drunk, and tea and coffee make you miserably drunk.

If you knew Spring in the old days, you wouldn't have known him towards the end—and I don't suppose he would have known you. For in his old age he was a Person. He was odd messenger at Thames Police Court. In November, 1898 Spring, who was then the local reprobate, took to heart the kindly abmonitions of Sir John Dickinson, then magistrate at Thames, and signed the pledge of total abstinence. Ever afterwards, on the anniversary of that great day, Spring would hand to the magistrate a poem in celebration of the fact that he had "kept off it" for another year.

I visited Spring just before his death in his lodging—lodging stranger than that of any Montmartre poet.

The Thames Police Court is in Arbour Square, Stepney, and Spring lived near his work. Through many mean streets I tracked his dwelling, and at last I found it. I climbed flights of broken stairs in a high forbidding house. I stumbled over steps and unexpected turns, and at last I stood with a puffy, red-faced, grey-whiskers, stocky old fellow, in a candle-lit garret whose one window looked over a furtively noisy court.

It was probably his family name of Waters that drove him to drink in his youth, since when, he has been known as the man who put the tea in "teetotal." In his room I noticed a bed of nondescript colour and make-up, a rickety chest of drawers (in which he kept his treasures), two doubtful chairs, a table, a basin, and bits of food strewn impartially everywhere. A thick, limp smell hung over all, and the place seemed set a-jigging by the flickering light of the candle.

There I heard his tale. He sat on the safe chair while I flirted with the other.

It was on the fortieth occasion that he yielded to Sir John Dickinson's remonstrances and signed the pledge, and earned the respect of all connected with that court where he had made so many appearances. All through that Christmas and New Year he had, of course, a thin time; it was suffocating to have to refuse the invitation: " Come on, Spring—let's drink your health!" But what did Spring do? Did he yield? Never. When he found he was thirsty, he sat down and wrote a poem, and by the time he had found a rhyme for Burton, the thirst had passed. Then, too, everybody took an interest in him and gave him work and clothes, and so on. Oh, yes, it's a profitable job being a reformed vagabond in Stepney.

He was employed on odd messages and errands for the staff at Thames Police Court, and visited the police-stations round about to do similar errands, such as buying breakfast for the unfortunates who have been locked up all night and are about to face the magistrate. Whatever an overnight prisoner wants in the way of food he may have (intoxicants barred), if he cares to pay for it, and Spring was the agile fellow who fetched it for him; and many stray coppers (money, not policemen) came his way.

All these things he told me as I sat in his mephitic lodging. Spring, like his brother Villon, was a man of all trades; no job was too "odd" for him to take on. Holding horses, taking messages from court to station, writing odes on this and that, opening and shutting doors, and dashing about in his eightieth year just like a newsboy—Spring was certainly a credit to Stepney. On my mentioning that I myself made songs at times, he dashed off the following impromptu, as I was falling down his crazy stairs at midnight:—

> Oh, how happy we all should be,
> If none of us ever drank anything stronger than tea.
> For how can a man hope to write a beautiful song
> When he is hanging round the public-houses all day long?

"Spring Onions" apart, Stepney is a home for all manner of queer characters, full of fire and salt; from Peter the Painter, of immortal memory, to those odd-job men who live well by being Jacks of all trades, and masters of them, too.

There are my good friends, Johnny, the scavenger, Mr. 'Opkinson, the cat's-meat man, 'Erb, the boney, Fat Fred, who keeps the baked-potato can, and that lovable personality "My Uncle Toby," gate-man at one of the docks.

There's 'Orace, too, the minder. Ever met him? Ever employed him? Probably not, but if you live near any poor market-place, and ever have occasion for his services, I cordially recommend him.

'Orace is the best minder east of the Pump. What does he mind? Your business, not his. Haven't you ever seen him at it in the more homely quarters? At a penny a time, it's good hunting; and 'Orace is the only man I know who blesses certain recent legislation.

His profession sprang from the Children Act, which debarred parents from taking children into public-houses. Now, there are thousands of respectable couples who like to have a quiet—or even a noisy—drink on market-night; and the effect of the Act was that they had to go in singly, one taking a drink while the other stood outside and held the baby.

There was 'Orace's opportunity, and he took it. Why not let father and mother take their drink together, while 'Orace sang lullabies to his Majesty?

Admirable idea. It caught on, for 'Orace has a

way with babies. He can talk baby guff by the hour, and in the whole of his professional career he has never had to mind a baby that did not "take" to him on sight.

The fee is frequently more than a penny. If the old dad wants to stay for a bit, he will stand 'Orace a drink (under the rose) and a pipe of 'baccy. Sundays and holidays are his best days. He selects his public-house, on the main road always, and works it all day. Often he has five or six kiddies at a time to protect; and he gave me a private tip towards success as a "minder": always carry a number of bright things in your pockets—nails, pearl buttons, bits of coloured chalk, or, best of all, a piece of putty.

Outside his regular pitch, the public-house owns a horse-trough, but as no horses now draw up, the trough is dry, and in this he places his half-dozen or so protégés, out of danger and as happy as you please.

Then there's Artie, the copper's nark. What shall be said of Artie? Shall I compare him to a summer's day? No, I think not; rather to a cob-webbed Stepney twilight. I don't commend Artie. Indeed, I have as little regard for him as I have for those poisonous weeds that float on the

Thames near Greenwich at flood. He is a thoroughly disagreeable person, with none of the acid qualities of the really bad man or the firelight glow of commonplace sinners like ourselves. He is incapable of following any other calling. He has been, from boyhood, mixed up with criminal gangs, but he has not the backbone necessary for following them on their enterprises. Always he has wanted to feel safe; so he cringes at the feet of officialism. He is hated by all—by the boys whose games he springs and by the unscrupulous police who employ him. His rewards are small: a few pence now and then, an occasional drink, and a tolerant eye towards his own little misbehavings.

Often the police are puzzled as to how Artie gets his information. If you were to ask him, he would become Orientally impassive.

" Ah, you'd like to know, wouldn't yer? "

But the truth is that he does not himself know. In a poor district—Walworth, Hoxton, or Notting Dale—everybody talks; and it is in these districts that Artie works. He is useless in big criminal affairs; he can only gather and report information on the petty doings of his associates. The moment any small burglary is planned, two or three people know about it, for the small burglar is always maladroit and ill-instructed in his methods, and is bound to confide in some one. Artie is always about like a pedatory bird to snatch up crumbs of other people's business.

Are you married, and were you married at a Registry Office? If so, it's certain that you've met my dear old friend, Stepney Syd, the Congratulator, one of our most earnest war-workers; as "unwearied" as Lady Dardy Dinkum.

Congratulations, spoken at the right moment, in the right way, to the right people, are a paying proposition. The war has made no difference in the value of those mellifluous syllables, unless it be in an upward direction. It's a soft job, too. Syd never works after three in the afternoon. He cannot, because his work is the concluding touch to the marriage service. It consists in hanging about registry-offices—that in Covent Garden is very popular with young people in a hurry—and waiting until a cab arrives with prospective bride and bridegroom. When they leave, Syd is there to open the door for them, and respectfully offer felicitations; and so fatuous and helpless is man when he has taken a woman for life that he dare not ignore this happy omen.

Thus, Syd comes home every time on a good thing, and, by careful watching of the weekly papers in the Free Library, and putting two and two together, he contrives, like some of our politicians, to anticipate events, and to be where the good things are.

Strolling round Montagu Street the other night, I met, in one of the little Russian cafés, a man who pitched me a tale of woe—a lean, ferrety little man, with ferrety eyes and fingers that urged me to button my overcoat and secure all pockets.

But I was shocked to discover that he was an honest man. Diamonds and honesty seldom walk hand-in-hand, and precious stones and virtue do not yet publicly kiss each other; and he talked so much of diamonds that my first apprehensions were perhaps justified. I learnt, however, that his was a sad case. He was a diamond-cutter by trade, and in those war days one might as usefully have diamonds in Amsterdam (as Maudi Darrell's song went) as have them in London.

I had not before met a man who so casually juggled with the symbols of revue-girlhood, so I bought him some more vodka and tea-and-lemon, and led him on to talk. Stones to the value of £20,000 passed through his hands every day, but none of them stuck. This fact greatly refreshed my dimming faith in human nature, until he qualified it by adding that it wasn't worth a cutter's while to steal. Every worker in the trade is known to every branch, and he would have no second chance.

Apprenticeship to the trade of diamond-cutting costs £200: and, once out of his indentures, the apprentice must join the Union, for it would be useless for him, however proficient in his business, to attempt to obtain a post without his Union ticket.

The diamond-mechanic earns anything from £3 to £8 per week. The work calls for a very considerable knowledge of the characters of stones, for very deft fingers, and for exceptionally shrewd judgment; since every diamond or brilliant, however minute, has sixty-four facets, each of which has to be made and polished on a lathe.

The stones are handed out in the workshop practically haphazard, and in the event of the loss of a stone, no disturbance is caused. The staff simply look for it; the floor of the shop is swept up with a fine broom, and the dust sifted until it is found. The explanation of this laxity is the International Diamond Cutters' Union.

In the process of diamond-cutting, of course, the stone loses about 60 per cent. of its weight; and the cutter told me that the fillings that come from the stone, mixed with the oil of the lathe, make the finest lubricant for a razor-strop. The making of his smooth cheeks was the perfect razor sharpened with diamond filings!

Before we parted, he showed me casually a green diamond. This is the most rare form of stone, and there are only six known examples in the world. No, he didn't steal it. It had just been handed to him for setting, and he was carrying it in his waistcoat-pocket in the careless manner of all stone-dealers.

After he and a sure thousand pounds had vanished into the night, I sat for awhile in the café listening to the chatter of the cigarette-girls of the quarter.

It was all of war. Of Stefan, who had been repatriated; of Abramovitch, who had evaded service by bolting to Ireland with a false green form for which he had paid £100; of Sergius, who had been hiding in a cellar.

When one thinks of cigarette-girls one thinks at

once of Marion Crawford's *Cigarette-maker's Romance* and of Martin Harvey's super-sentimental performance in that play, so dear to the Streatham flapper. But Sonia Karavitch, though soaked in the qualities of her race—dark beauty, luxurious curls, brooding temper, and spiritual melancholy—would, I fear, repel those who only know her under the extravagantly refining rays of the limelight. But those who love humanity in the raw will love her.

Sonia Karavitch is seventeen. She wears a black frock, with many sprigs of red ribbon at her neck and in her raven hair. Her fingers are stained brown with tobacco; but, though she has heavy eyes and lounges languorously, like a drowsy cat in the sunshine, she works harder than most other factory-girls.

From six o'clock in the morning until eight o'clock at night she is at her table, rolling by the thousand those hand-made cigarettes which command big prices in Piccadilly. When she speaks she has a lazy voice with a curious lisp, and it is full of sadness.

Yet she is not sad. She has a pleasant little home in one of the big tenements, where she lives with her mother and little brother, and, in her own demonstrative way, is happy. The harder she works, the more money there is for luxuries for the little brother. Often of an evening her friends come home with her, and drink tea-and-lemon with her, and make music.

Sonia Karavitch is very shy, and never mixes with the folk who are not of her own colony. She was born in Stepney of Russian parents, and she never goes out of Stepney. And why should she? For in the half-dozen streets where she lives her daily life she can speak the language of her parents, can buy clothes such as her mother wore in Odessa, and can find all those little touches that mean home to the homeless or the exiled.

Every morning she goes straight to the factory; at noon she goes home to dinner; and in the evening she goes straight home again. Sometimes on Saturday afternoons—which is her Sunday, for Sonia is of Jewish faith—she takes a walk in Whitechapel High Street, because, you see, there is much life in Whitechapel High Street; there are her compatriots, and there are street-organs, and violets are a penny a bunch.

When she has had a good week she sometimes takes her mother and brother for kvass to one of the many Russian restaurants in Osborn Street and Little Montagu Street.

Sometimes you see Sonia Karavitch at a table, sipping her tea, and listening to the talk, and you may wonder why that sad, far-away look in her eyes. She is not in Stepney. Her soul has flown to her native land—to the steppes, to the cold airs of Russia, whither a certain Russian lad, who used to work by her side in the cigarette factory in Osborn Street, was dispatched by a repatriation order.

But then she remembers mother and little brother, and stops her dreamings, and hurries on to work.

Many wild folk have sat in these cafés and discoursed on the injustices of civilization; and at one time private presses in the neighbourhood gave forth inflammatory sheets bearing messages from international warriors in the cause of freedom.

If ever you are tired of the solemn round of existence, don't take a holiday at the seaside, don't go to the war. Edit an anarchist news-sheet, and your life will be full of quick perils and alarms.

Another of my Stepney friends is Jane, the flower-girl, who tramps every day from Stepney to Covent Garden, and sells her stock from a pitch near Leicester Square. Here's another ardent war-worker.

Some worthy people may not think that the selling of violets comes properly under the fine exclusive label of War Work; but these are the neurotics whose only idea of doing their bit is that of twisting their soiling fingers about anything that carries a message of grace; who fume at a young man because he isn't in khaki, and, when he is in uniform, kill him with a look because he isn't in hospital blue, and, when he is in hospital, regard him askance because he isn't eager to go back.

"Flowers!" they snort or wheeze. "Fiddling with flowers in war-time! It ought to be stopped. Look at the waste of labour. Look at the press on transport. Will the people never realize," etc.

Yet, good troglodytes, because the world is at war, shall we then wipe from the earth everything that links us, however lightly, to God—and save Germany the trouble? Must everything be lead and steel? Old Man—dost thou think, because thou art old, that glory and loveliness have passed away with the corroding of thy bones?

Nay, youth shall still take or make its pleasure; fair girls shall still adorn their limbs with silks, and flowers shall still be sweet to the nose.

Old Man—on many occasions when I could get no food—not even war-bread—the sight and smell of bunches of violets have furnished sustenance for mind and body. So fill thy belly, if thou wilt, with the waxy potato; put the Army cheese where the soldier puts the pudding; shovel into thy mouth the frozen beef and offal that may renew thy energies for further war-work; but, if there be any grace of God still left in thee, if there be any virtue, any charity—leave, for those who are shielding thy senescent body, the flower-girls about Piccadilly Circus on a May morning.

"Vi'lerts! Swee' Vi'lerts! Pennyer bunch!"

Good morning, Jane! How sweet you and your violets look in the tangle of traffic that laces and interlaces itself about Alfred Gilbert's Mercury.

Morning by morning, fair or foggy, she stands by the fountain; and if you give her more than a passing glance you will note that her tumbled hair is of just the right shade of red, and in her eyes are the very violets that she holds to your indifferent nose, and under her lucent skin beat the imperious pulses of youth.

Jane is fourteen, and Jane is always smiling; not because she is fourteen, but because it's such fun to be alive and to be selling flowers. Indeed, she looks herself like a little posy, sweet and demure. Times may be bad, but they are not reflected in Jane's appearance.

Of education she has only what the Council School gave her in the odd hours when she choose to attend; of religion she has none, but she has a philosophy of her own, which, in a sentence, is To Get All The Fun You Can Out of Things.

That's why Jane's smile is a smile that certain people look for every morning as they alight from their bus in the Circus. But you must not imagine that Jane is good in the respectable sense of the word. Let anyone annoy her, or try to "dish" her of one of her customers. Then, when it comes to back-chat, Jane can more than hold her own in the matter of language; and once I saw an artillery officer's face turn livid during a discussion between her and a rival flower-girl.

The war has hit Jane very badly. The young bloods who frequented her stall in the old days, and bought the most expensive buttonholes every morning, are now in khaki, and a thoughtless Army Order forbids an officer to decorate his tunic with a spray of carnations or a moss-rose.

There are only the old bounders remaining, and their custom depends so much on such a number of things—the morning's news, the fact that they are not ten years younger, the weather, and the state of their digestions.

Jane always reads the paper before she starts work, because, as she says, then you know what to expect. She doesn't believe in meeting trouble halfway, but she believes in being prepared for it. When there's good news, stout old gentlemen will buy a bunch of violets for themselves, and perhaps a cluster of blossoms for the typist. But when the news is bad, nobody is in the mood for flowers. They want to band themselves together and tell one another how awful it is; which, as Jane says, is all wrong.

"If they'd only buy a bunch of violets and stick it in their coats, other people would feel better by looking at them, and they'd forget the bad news in the jolly old smell in their buttonhole."

Yes, Jane's fourteen years have given her much wisdom, and she is doing as fine war-work as any admiral or field-marshal.

While in Stepney we mustn't forget good Mrs. Joplin. Mrs. Joplin lives up a narrow court of menacing aspect, and in her window is a printed card, bearing the cryptic legend—" Mangling Done Here "—which, to an American friend of mine, suggested that atrocities of a German kind were going on downstairs. But I calmed his fears by assuring him that Mrs. Joplin's business card was a simple indication of her willingness to receive from her neighbours bundles of newly-washed clothes, and put them through a machine called a mangle, from which they were discharged neatly pressed and folded. The remuneration for this service is usually but a few coppers—beer-money, nothing more; so to procure the decencies of existence Mrs. Joplin lets her basement rooms for—What's that? Yes, I daresay you've had a few pewter half-crowns and florins passed on you lately, but what's that to do with me—or Mrs. Joplin? Do you want me to suggest that good Mrs. Joplin is a twister; a snide-merchant? Never let it be said. Good Mrs. Joplin, unlike so many of her neighbours, has never seen the inside of a police-court, much less a prison.

Speaking of prisons, it was in Stepney that I was told how to carry myself if ever I came within the grip of the law on frequent occasions. The English prison is not an establishment to which one turns with anticipation of happiness; but there is one prison which is as good as a home of rest for those suffering from the pain of the world. There is but one condition of eligibility: you must be a habitual criminal.

If you fulfilled that condition, you were dispatched to the Camp Hill Detention Prison in the Isle of Wight.

A most comfortable affair, this Camp Hill. It stands in pleasant grounds, near Newport; and the walls are not the grey, scowling things that enclose Holloway, or Reading, or Wandsworth, but walls of warm brown stone, such as any good fellow of reputable fame might build about his mansion. Close-shaven lawns and flower-beds delight the eye, and the cells are roomy apartments with real windows. The guests do not dine in solitude; they are marched together to the dining-hall, and there nourished, not with skilly or stew, with its hunk of bread and a pewter platter, but with meat and plum-duff, sometimes fish, greenstuffs, and cocoa. This, of course, in peacetime; the menu has no doubt suffered variations in these latter days. The tables are covered. After the meal the good fellows may sit for a few minutes and enjoy a pipe of tobacco, even as the respectable citizen. A fair number of marks for good behaviour carries with it the privilege of smoking after the night meal as well, and one of the most severe punishments is the docking of this smoking privilege.

Also, a canteen is provided. Not only do they wallow in luxury; they are paid for it. Twopence a day is given to each prisoner for exceptional conduct, and one penny of this may be spent at the canteen. This is by way of payment for work done—the work being of a much lighter kind than that given to ordinary " second division " prisoners. In cases where conduct fulfils every expectation of the authorities, the good lad is rewarded, every six months, with a stripe. Six stripes entitle the holder to a cash reward, half of which he may spend, the other half being banked. The canteen sells sweets, mineral waters, cigarettes, apples, oranges, nuts etc. Those inclined to the higher forms of nourishment may use the library. There are current magazines, novels of popular " healthy " writers (it would be unfair to give their names; they might not appreciate the epithet), and—uplifting thought—the works of

Spencer, Huxley, Darwin, and some French highbrows.

On special occasions bioscope shows of an educative kind are given. Oh, I do love my virtue, but I wish I were a habitual criminal. Why wasn't I born in Stepney, and born a vagabond?

Whether the prison is still running on the old lines I know not. Most likely the British habitual convicts have been served with ejectment notices to make room for German prisoners. I wouldn't wonder.

THE KIDS' MAN

"I'll learn yeh, y' little wretch!"

"Oowh! Don't—don't!"

The lady, savagely wielding a decayed carpet-beater, bent over the shrinking form of the child—a little storm of short skirts and black hair. Her arm ached and her face steamed, but she continued to shower blows wherever she could get them in, until suddenly the storm limply subsided into a small figure which doubled up and fell.

A step sounded in the doorway, and the lady looked up, frayed at the edges and panting. A small, slight man, in semi-official dress, stood just inside the room, which gave directly on to a byway of Homerton.

"Na then, Feet—mind yer dirty boots on my carpet, cancher? What's the——"

"N.S.P.C.C.," replied Feet. He stooped over the child, lifted her, and set her on a slippery sofa. "Had my eye on you for some time. Thought there were something dicky with this child."

" 'Ere, look 'ere—I mean, can't 'er muvver 'it 'er—— "

" Steady, please. Let me warn you—— "

The lady threatened with glances, but Kids' Man met them.

She fumed. " Ow! You waltz in, do yeh? Well, strikes me yeh'll waltz out quicker'n yeh came in. 'Ere—Arfer! " Her raucous voice scraped up the narrow stairway leading from the room, and in answer came a misty voice, suggesting revelries by night. The lady roared again: " Ar-ferr! Get up an' come daown. 'Ere's a little swab insultin' yer wife! Kids' Man insultin' yer wife! "

Kids' Man made no move, but stood over the sofa with sober face, ministering to the heavily breathing bundle. Overhead came bumps and a prayer for delivery from women.

Then on the lower step of the stairway appeared a symbol of Aurora in velveteen breeches and a shirt of indeterminate colour. His braces hung dolefully at the rear as he bleared on the situation. His furry head moved from side to side. " Wodyeh want me t'do? "

" Cosh 'im! Insultin' yer wife! "

He stared. Then his lip moved and he grinned. He hitched up his trousers, belted them with braces, and expectorated on both hands with gusto. "Git aout, else I'll split yer faice!"

No answer. "Righto!" He descended from the stair, and, hands down, fists closed, chin protruded, advanced on the bending Inspector with that slow, insidious movement proper to street-fighters. "Won't git aout, woncher? Grrr—yeh!"

Kids' Man looked up and met him with a steady stare. But the stare annoyed him, so he lifted up his fist and smote Kids' Man between the eyes. Then things happened. He towered over the Inspector. "Want another?" The Inspector lifted a short and apparently muscleless arm.

Bk! Aurora reeled as the fist met his jaw, and was followed by a swift one under the ear. For a moment astonishment seemed to hold him as he bleared at the slight figure; then he seemed about to burst with wrath; then he became a cold sportsman. The wife screamed for aid.

"Aoutside—come on!" He shoved Kids' Man before him into the walk, which, torpid a moment ago, now flashed with life and movement.

Quickly the auditorium was filled with a moist, unlovely crowd of sloppy rags and towzled heads. While Kids' Man ministered to his nose, Arfer hitched his trousers, fingered his shirt-sleeves, and talked in staccato to his seconds, about a dozen in number. The crowd grunted and grinned. It seemed evident that Kids' Man was about to get it in the neck. One or two went to his side as he quietly turned back his sleeves, not for purposes of encouragement, but merely in order to preserve the correct niceties of the scrap.

A light tap on the body from either party, and then more things happened. "Go it, Arfer, flatten 'im! Cosh 'im! Rip 'im back, Arfer. Give 'im naughty-naughty, Arfer!"

But, as the crowd scraped and shuffled this way and that, they gave a panicky clearing to a spry retreat by Kids' Man. He was done for; Arfer was chasing him. They capered and chi-iked. Then, with a smart turn, he landed beautifully on the point, and sent the pursuing Arfer flat to the ground. The crowd murmured and oathfully exhorted Arfer to fink what he was doin' of. Flatten the Kids' Man—that was his job. They met again, and this time the Society received one on the mouth and another on the nose. He sat heavily down, and his seconds flashed wet handkerchiefs. The crowd cheered.

" 'Ad enough? "

But with a sudden spurt he came up again. His right landed on Arfer's nose, a natty upper-cut followed it. He got in another with his right, and pressed his man. The lady screamed, and disregarding the ethics of the ring, splurged in and seized the Society's coat-tails. But the crowd begged her to desist. Then the child, who, with the toughness of her class, had found her legs again, flitted fearfully about the fringe of the crowd.

" Wade in, mister! 'It the old woman—fetch 'er a swipe across the snitch! "

Now Kids' Man began to take an interest in the affair. Dodging a swinging blow of his lumbering opponent, he got in a half-arm jab. They closed, and embraced each other, and swayed, and the crowd chanted " Dear Old Pals." For a moment they strained; then Kids' Man lifted his enemy bodily held him, and with a peculiar twist dropped him. He lay still. . . .

A murmur of wonder swelled quickly to a broad roar. The crowd surged in, squirming and hustling. For a moment it seemed that Kids' Man would get torn. It was just a hair's-breadth question between lynching, and triumphal chairing. The sporting spirit prevailed, and: " Raaay! Good on yeh, mate! Well done th' S'ciety!" The lads swung in and gathered admiringly around the victor, who tenderly caressed a damaged beetroot of a face, while half a dozen helpers impeded each other's efforts to render first aid to the prostrate Arfer.

"Where's the blankey twicer? Lemme git 'old of 'im. Lemme git 'old of 'im!" implored the lady. But she was no longer popular, and they hustled her aside, so that in impotent rage she smote her prostrate husband with her foot for failing to uphold her honour before a measly little Kids' Man what she could have torn in two wiv one hand.

"Well, 'e's gotter nerve, ain't 'e?"

"Firs' chap ever I knew stand up t'old Arfer. Fac'!"

"Yerce—'e's—e's gotter nerve!"

"Tell yeh what I say, boys—three cheers for th' Kids' Man!"

And as the bruised and discoloured Kids' Man gripped the hand of Orphan Dora and led her, brave with new importance, from the Walk to

THE KIDS' MAN

headquarters, a round of beery cheering made sweet music in their rear.

"Well, fancy a little chap like that. . . . Well, 'e's gotter blasted nerve!"

* * * * *

The Kids' Man. That is his title—used sometimes affectionately and sometimes bitterly. He is the children's champion, and often he is met with curses, and that plea of parenthood which is supposed to justify all manner of gross and unnameable abominations: "Can't a farver do what he likes wiv his own child?"

The Society employs two hundred and fifty Inspectors, whose work is to watch over the welfare of the children in their allotted district. But, since most ill-treatment takes place behind closed doors, it is difficult for an outsider to obtain direct evidence, and neighbours, even when they know that children are being starved and daily tortured, are shy of lodging information, lest it may lead to the publicity of the police-court and the newspapers, and subsequently to open permanent enmity from the people next whom they have to live.

The Kids' Man is usually an old Army or Navy man, accustomed to making himself heard, and able to hold his own. The chief qualities for such a post are: a real love of children; tact and knowledge of men; and ability to deal with a hostile reception. It is by no means pleasant, as you have seen, to pay a warning visit to a house up a narrow alley, whose inhabitants form something of a clan or freemasonry lodge.

The motto of the Society, however, is persuasion. Prosecutions are extremely distasteful, and are only used when all other means have failed. In any case that comes to the Inspector's knowledge, his first thought is the children's well-being. If they are being starved, he provides them with food, clothes, bedding and baths, or sees that the parish does so without any of the delays incident to parish charity. Then he has a quiet talk with the parents, and gives a warning. Usually this is enough. In cases where the neglect is due to lack of work, he is sometimes an employment agency, and finds work for the father. But, if necessary, there are more warnings, and then, with great reluctance, an appearance in court is called for.

Cruelty is of two kinds—active and passive. The passive cruelty is the cruelty of neglect—lack of proper food, clothing, sanitation, etc. The other kind—the active cruelty of a diabolical nature—comes curiously enough, not so much from the lower, but from the upper classes. It is seldom that the rough navvy is deliberately cruel to his children; but Inspectors can tell you some appalling stories of torture inflicted on children by leisured people of means and breeding. Among their convictions are doctors, lawyers, clergymen, and many women of position.

There was one terrible case of a woman in county society—you will remember her Cornish name—who had been guilty of atrocious cruelty to a little girl of twelve. The Kids' Man called. The woman maintained that a mother had a perfect right to correct her own child. She called the child and fondled it to prove that rumour of tortures was wrong. But the Kids' Man knows children; and the look in the child's eyes told him of terrorizing. He demanded a medical examination.

The case was proved in court. A verdict of "Guilty" was given. And the punishment for this fair degenerate—£50 fine! The punishment for the Kids' Man was a kind of social ostracism. There lies the difficulty of the work. The woman's position had saved her.

The Kids' Man needs to have his eyes open

everywhere and at every time for signs of suffering among the little ones. And often, where a father won't listen to advice from him, he is found amenable to suggestions from Mrs. Inspector.

In every big town in this country you will find the N.S.P.C.C. bureau, but, in spite of their efforts, too much cruelty is going on that might be stopped if the British people, as a race, were not too fond of "minding their own business" and shutting their eyes to everyday evils.

If you still think England a Christian and enlightened country, you had better accompany an N.S.P.C.C. man on his daily round. Before you do so, inspect the record at their offices. Read the verbatim reports of some of their cases. Look at their "museum" which Mr. Parr, the secretary, will show you; a museum more hideous than any collection of inquisition relics or than anything in the Tower. You will then know something of the hideous conditions of child-life in "this England of ours," and you will be prepared for what you shall see on your tour with the Kids' Man.

CROWDED HOURS

WHAT does the Cockney's mind first register when, far from home, he visualizes the London that he loves with the casual devotion of his type? To the serious tourist London is the shrine of England's history; to the ordinary artist, who sees life in line and colour, it is a city of noble or delicate " bits "; to the provincial it is a playground; to the business man a market; but to the Cockney it is one big club, odourous of the goodly fellowship that blossoms from contact with human-kind.

" Far from the madding crowd " may express the longings of the modern Simeon Stylites, but your Cockney is no Simeon. He doesn't pray to be put upon an island where the crowds are few. The thicker the crowd, the more elbows that delve into his ribs, the hotter the steam of human-kind, the happier he is. Far from the madding crowd be blowed! Man's place, he holds, is among his fellows; and he sniffs with contempt at this widespread desire to escape from other people. To him it is a sign of an unhealthy mind, if not pure blasphemy.

So, when he thinks of London, he does not think of a city of palaces, or serene architectural triumphs; of a huckster's mart or a playground. At the word "London" he sees people: the crowds in the Strand, in Walworth Road, Lavender Hill, Whitechapel Road, Camden Town High Street.

Your moods may be various, and London will respond. You may work, you may idly dream away the hours, or you may actively enjoy yourself in play; but if you wish that supreme enjoyment—the enjoyment of other people—then London affords opportunities in larger measure than any city that I know.

I discovered the magic and allure of crowds when I was fourteen years old and worked as office-boy in those filthy alleys marked in the Postal Directory as "E.C." Streets and crowds became my refreshment and entertainment then, and my palate is not yet blunted to their savour. I do not want the flowery mead or the tree-covered lane or the insect-ridden glade—at least, not for long; and I hate that dreadful hollow behind the little wood. Give me six o'clock in the evening and a walk from the City to Oxford Circus, through the soft Spring or the darkling Autumn, with festive feet whispering all around you, and your heart filled with that grey-green romance which is London.

Once out of Newgate Street and across Holborn Viaduct I was happy, for I was, so to speak, in a foreign country; so wholly different were the people of Holborn from the people of Cheapside. The crowds of the City had always to me, a mean, craven air about them. They walked homeward with lagging steps and worn faces. They seemed always preoccupied with paltry problems. They carried the stamp of their environment: a dusty market-place, in which things made by more adept hands and brains are passed from wholesale place to wholesale place with sorry bargaining on the odd halfpenny.

But West and West Central were a pleasuance of the finer essences, and involuntarily body and soul assumed there a transient felicity of gait. One walked and thought suavely. There were noble shops, brilliant theatres, dainty restaurants, highways whose sole business was pleasure, rent with gay lights and oh! so many delightful people. At restaurant and theatre doors one might pause pensively and touch finger-tips, as it were, with rose-leaf grace and beauty and fine comradeship; a refreshing exercise after encounters with the sordid and the uncouth in Gracechurch Street. Then, when the hoofs clattered and the motors hooted and the whistles blew, and streets were drenched with festal light and festal folk, I was, I felt, abroad. Figure to yourself that you are walking through the streets of Teheran, or Stamboul, or Moscow, surrounded by strange bazaars and people who seem to have stepped from some book of magic so far removed are they from your daily interests. So did I feel as I walked down Piccadilly. It was suffocating to think that there were so many streets to explore, so many types to meet and to know. I wanted then to make heaps and heaps of friends—not, I must confess, for friendship—but just for the sake of meeting people who did interesting and gracious things, and for the sake of knowing that I *had* a host of friends. The plashing of the fountains in Trafalgar Square, the lights of the Alhambra and Empire seen through the green trees of Leicester Square, the procession of 'buses along Holborn and Oxford Streets, the alluring teashops of Piccadilly and the scornful opulence of the hotels—these things sank into me and became part of me.

My way to the City lay through Leicester Square, and the morning crowd in that quarter bears for me still the same charm. On a bright Spring day it might be Paris. There is a sense of space and sparkle about it. The little milliners' girls, in piquant frocks, evoke memories of Louise, and the crowding curls on their cheeks waft a perfume of youth-time lyrics, chiming softly against the more strident and repulsively military garb of the girl porters and doorkeepers. The cleaners, bustling about the steps of the music-halls, throw adumbrations of entertainment on the morning streets. People are leisurely busy in an agreeable way—not the huckstering E.C. way.

In Piccadilly Circus there is the same sense of light and song among the crowds emerging from the Tube. The shops are decked in all the colours of the Maytime, and not one little workgirl but pauses to throw a mute appeal to the posturing silks and laces and pray that the lily-wristed, wanton damsel of Fortune will turn a hand in her direction.

But in the City, as I have said, there is little of this delight to be found, either at morning, noon or night. The typical crowd of this district may be seen at London Bridge, where, from eight to half-past ten in the morning and from half-past five to half-past seven in the evening, the dispirited toilers swarm to or from work. Indeed, it is not a crowd: it is a *cortège*, marching to the obsequies of hope and fear. It is a funeral march of marionettes. Here are no gay colours; no smiles; no persiflage. All is sombre. Even the typists and the little workgirls make no effort towards bright raiment; all is dingy and soiled, not with the clean dirt that hangs about the barges and wharves on the river, but with the mustiness of old ledgers and letter-files. Listless in the morning and taciturn in the evening are these people; and to watch them for an hour from the windows of the Bridge House Hotel is to suffer an attack of spiritual dyspepsia. For, among them, are men who have crossed that bridge twice daily for thirty years, walking always on the same side, always at the same pace, and arriving at the other end at precisely the same minute. There are men who began that daily journey with bright boyish faces, clean collars, and their first bowler hats, brave with the importance of working in the City. Their hearts were fired with dreams and ambition. They had heard tales of office-boys who, by industry, had been taken eventually into partnership. They received their first rise. Later, they achieved the romantic riches of thirty shillings a week. They made the acquaintance of a girl in their suburban High Street. They married. And now, at forty-five, all ambition gone, they are working in the same murky corner of the same office, and maintaining wife and child on three pounds a week. Their trousers are frayed and bag at the knees. Their coats are without nap or grace. Two collars a week suffice. Gone are the shining dreams. They have "settled down," without being conscious of the fact, and will make that miserable journey, with other sombre and silent phantoms, until the end. Verily, the London Bridge crowd of respectables is the most tragic of all London crowds, and the bridge itself a *via dolorosa*.

I do not know why work in the City should produce a more deadening effect on the souls of the workers than work in other quarters, but the fact that it does is recognized by all students of Labour conditions. I have worked in all quarters, and have noticed a curious change of outlook when I moved from the City to Fleet Street, or from Fleet Street to Piccadilly. You shall notice it, too, in the faces of the lunch-time crowds. East of St. Paul's, the note is apathy. Coming westward, just to Fleet Street, you perceive a change. Here boys and girls, men and women, seem to take an interest in things; one understands that they like their work. They do not regard it as a mere routine, to be dragged through somehow until the clock releases them.

A similar study in crowd psychology awaits you at the Tube stations in the early hours of the evening, when the rush is on. With elbows wedged into your ribs, and strange hot breaths pouring down your neck, you need all the serenity you have stored against such contingencies; and the attitude of the other people about you can mitigate your distress or enhance it. The City and South London crowd is not the kind of crowd that can bear its own troubles cheerfully, or help others to bear theirs. I would never wish to go on a day's holiday with any of its people. Their composite frame of mind is one of weak anger, expressive of "Why isn't Something Done? What's the use of going on like this?"

More comely is the St. James's Park or Westminster crowd. From five to half-past six these stations receive a steady stream of sweet and merry little girls from the mushroom Government Departments that have spawned all about this quarter. It is girls, girls, girls, all the way, with the feeble and the aged of the male species toiling behind.

On the Bakerloo you find a crowd that is—well, " rorty " is the only word. The people here are mostly southbound for the Elephant and Castle; and you know the Elephant and Castle and its warm, impetuous life. There are bold youths who have not fallen, like their fathers, to the cajolery of a collar-and-cuff job in the City, but have taken up the work that offers the best pecuniary reward. Grimy youths they are, but full of vitality, and they pour down the staircase in a Niagara of humanity.

An excellent centre for observing the varying moods of the evening crowd is Villiers Street, that gentle slope from which you may reach Charing Cross Station, the Hampstead Tube, the District Railway, or the Embankment trams. It is a finely mixed company, for, as any Londoner will tell you, the residents of the hundred suburbs differ from one another in manner, accent and appearance, even as the natives of different continents. Those who are using the Hampstead Tube are sharply marked from those who are taking the Embankment car to Clapham Junction; while those who are journeying on the South-Eastern to Croydon have probably never heard of Upton Park, whither the District will carry others. There are well-dressed people and ill-dressed people; some who are going home to soup, fish, a *soufflé* and coffee, with wine and liqueurs; and some who are going home to "tea," at about eight o'clock—bread-and-margarine and bloater paste, with a pint of tea, or, occasionally, a bit of tripe and onions. There are people in a mad hurry, and others who move in aloof idleness. And above them all stand the stalwart Colonials, waiting until 6.30, when the bars shall open, airily inspecting the troops of girls and comparing notes.

"Say now, jes' watch here. Here comes a real Fanny."

"Ah, gwan. I ain' got no time for Fannies. I finished wid 'em. Gimme beer, every time."

I have often wanted to make a song of Villiers Street, but I have never been able to catch just the essence of its atmosphere. I am sure, though, that the modern orchestra offers opportunities for one of our new composers to embrace it in an overture. No effort has been made, so far as I know, to interpret in music the noisy soul of the London crowds. Elgar's "Cockaigne" overture and Percy Grainger's "Handel in the Strand" were both retrospective in spirit, and the real thing yet remains to be done. It has been done on the Continent by Suppé ("Morning, Noon and Night in Vienna"), by Sibelius in his "Finlandia," by Massenet in his "Southern Town," and by Dvorák in "Carneval Roman." I await with eagerness a "Morning, Noon and Night at Charing Cross," scored by a born Cockney.

SATURDAY NIGHT

THE origins of Saturday night, as a social institution, are obscure. No doubt a little research would discover them to the earnest seeker, but I am temperamentally averse from anything like research. It is tedious in process and disappointing in result. Successful research means grasping at the reality and dropping the romance.

The outstanding fact about Saturday night is that it is an exclusively British institution. Neither America nor the Continent knows its precious joys. It is one of the few British institutions that reconcile me to being an islander. It is a festival that is observed with the same casual ritual in the London slums and in Northumberland mining villages; in Scottish hills and in the byways of the Black Country; in Camden Town High Street and in the hamlets of the Welsh marches. Certainly, so long as my aged elders can carry their memories, and the memories of their fathers before them, Saturday night has been a festival recognized in all homely homes. Strange that it has only once been celebrated in literature.

It is, as it were, a short grace before the meal of leisure offered by the Sabbath; a side-dish before the ample banquet; a trifling with the olives of sweet idleness. On Saturday night the cares of the week are, for a space, laid aside, and men and women gather with their kind for amiable chatter and such mild conviviality as the times may afford. Then the bonds of preoccupation are loosed, and men escape for dalliance with the lighter things of life. Then the good gossips in town and country take their sober indulgence in the social amenities. In village street, or raucous town highway, they will pause between shops to greet this or that neighbour and discuss affairs of mutual concern.

On Saturday night is kept the festival of the String Bag, one of those many rigid feasts of the people that find no place in the Kalendar of the Prayer Book. Go where you will about the country on this night, and you will witness the celebration of this good domestic saint by the cheerful and fully choral service of Shopping. Go to East Street (Walworth Road); to St. John's Road (Battersea); to Putney High Street; to Stratford Broadway; to Newington Butts; to Caledonian Road; to Upper Street (Islington); to Norton-

Folgate; to Kingsland Road; to Salmon Lane (Limehouse); to Mare Street (Hackney); to the Electric Avenue (Brixton); to Powis Street (Woolwich); to the great shopping centres of provincial cities or to the easier market-places of the rural district, and you will find this service lustily in progress; the shops lit with a fresh glamour for this their special occasion. You will taste a something in the air—a sense of well-being, almost of carnival—that marks this night from other nights of the week. You will see Mother hovering about the shops and stalls, her eye peeled for the elusive bargain, while Father, or one of the children, stands away off with the bag; and when the goodwife has achieved all that she set out to do, and the string bag is distended like an overfed baby, then comes the crowning joy of the feast, when the shoppers slip together into the private bar of the " Green Dragon " or the " White Horse," and compare notes with other Saturday-nighters and condemn the beer.

Saturday night is also, in millions of homes, Bath Night; another of the pious functions of this festival; and for this ceremony the attendance of the heads of the household is compulsory. Then the youngsters, according to their natures, howl

SATURDAY NIGHT

with delight or alarm as their turn for the tub approaches. They will be scrubbed by Mother and dried by Father; and when the whole brood is well and truly bathed and packed off to bed, the elders will depart with the string bag, and perchance, if shopping be expeditiously accomplished, take it, well-filled, to the second house of the local Empire or Palace.

Do you not remember—unless you were so unfortunate as to be brought up in what are called well-to-do surroundings—do you not remember the tingling delight that was yours when, to ensure correct behaviour during the week, the prospect was dangled before you of going shopping on Saturday night? Many Saturday nights do I recall, chiefly by association with these shopping expeditions, when I was permitted to carry the string bag; and the shopping expeditions again are recalled through the agency of smell. Never does my memory work so swiftly as when assisted by the nose; I am a bit of a dog in that way. When I catch the hearty smell of a provision shop, I leap back twenty-five years and I see the tempestuous Saturday-evening lights of Lavender Hill from the altitude of three-foot-six; and I remember how I would catalogue shop smells in my mind. There were the solemn smell of the furniture shop; the wholesome smell of the oilshop; the pungent smell of the chemist's; the potent smell of the "Dog and Duck," where I received my weekly heart-cake; the stiff smell of the linen-drapers'; the overpowering odour of the boot-shop, and the aromatic perfume of the grocer's; all of which, in one grand combination, present the smell of Saturday night: a smell as sharp and individual as the smell of Sunday morning or the smell of early-closing afternoon in the suburbs. If Rip van Winkle were to awake in any town or village on Saturday night, he would need no calendar to name for him the day of the week: the smell, the aspect, and the temper of the streets would surely inform him.

But lately Saturday night has come under control, and the severe hand of authority has wrenched away the most of its delight. Not now may the String Baggers express their individuality in shopping. Having registered for necessary comestibles at a given shop, they enjoy no more the sport of bargain-hunting, or of setting rival tradesmen in cheerful competition. Not now may the villagers crowd the wayside station for their single weekly railway trip to the neighbouring town, where was larger scope for the perfect shopper than the native village could afford. No more may the earnest London Saturday-nighter journey by tram or bus to outlying markets because the quality of the meat was better in that district than in his own, or the price of eggs a penny lower—though, if the truth be known, these facts were mostly proffered as excuse for the excursion. No more do residents of Brixton travel to Clapham Junction for their Sunday stores, or the elegant ones of Streatham slink guiltily to Walworth Road. No more is Hampstead seen chaffering at the stalls of Camden Town, or Bayswater struggling gallantly about the shops of the Edgware Road and Kilburn.

The main function of Saturday night has died a dismal death. Still, the social side remains. Shopping of a sort still has to be done. One may still meet one's cronies in the market streets, and compare the bulk and quality of one's ration of this and that, and take a draught of insipid ale at the "Blue Pigeon," and talk of the untowardness of the times. But half of the savour is gone out of the week's event; and it is well that the Scots peasant made his song about it before it was controlled.

RENDEZVOUS

ALTHOUGH London possesses a thousand central points suitable for a street rendezvous, Londoners seem to have decided by tacit agreement to use only five of these for their outdoor appointments. They are: Charing Cross Post Office, Leicester Square Tube, Piccadilly Tube, under the Clock at Victoria, and Oxford Circus Tube; and I have never known my friends telephone me for a meeting and fix a rendezvous outside this list. Indeed, I can now, by long experience, place the habits and character of casual acquaintances who wish to meet me, from their choice among these places.

Thus, a Charing Cross Post Office appointment means a pleasure appointment. Here, at one o'clock on Saturday afternoon, wait the bright girls and golden boys, their faces, like living lamps, shining through the cloud of pedestrians as a signal for that one for whom they wait. And, though you be late in keeping the appointment, you may be certain that the waiting party will be in placid mood. There is so much to distract and delight you on this small corner. There are the bustle of the Strand and the stopping buses; the busy sweep of Trafalgar Square, so spacious that its swift stream of traffic suggests leisure; the hot smell of savouries rising from the kitchens of Morley's Hotel; and the cynical amusement to be drawn from a study of the meetings and encounters of other waiting folk. Hundreds of appointments have I kept at Charing Cross Post Office. I have met soldier-friends there, after an absence of three years. I have met cousins and sisters and aunts, and damsels who stood not in any of these relations. And I have met the Only One there, many, many times; often happily; often in trepidation; and sometimes in lyrical ecstasy, as when a quarrel and a long parting have received the benison of reconciliation. Now, I can never pass the Post Office without a tremor, for its swart, squat exterior is, for me, bowered with delicious thrills.

Never keep an appointment under the Clock at Victoria. A meeting here is fatal to the sweetness of the intercourse that is to follow. Always he or she who arrives first will be peevish or irate by the time the second party turns up; for Victoria Station, with its lowering roof, affects you with a frightful sense of being shut in and smothered. Turn how you will, sharply or gently, and you cannon with some petulant human, and, retiring apologetically from him, you impale your kidney region on some fool's walking-stick or umbrella. That fool asks you to look where you're going, and then he gets his from a truckload of luggage. You laugh—bitterly. After three minutes of waiting in that violet-tinted beehive, you loathe your fellow-man; you loathe the entire animal kingdom. You " come over in one of them prickly 'eats." Your nerves flap about you like bits of bunting, and the new spring suit that set in such fine lines seems fit only for scaring birds. Then your friend arrives, and God help him if he's late!

I have watched these Victoria appointments many times while waiting for my train. The first party to the contract arrives, glances at the clock, and strolls to the bookstall, cheerfully swinging stick or umbrella. He strolls back to the clock, glances, compares it with his watch. Hums a bar or two. Coughs. A flicker of dismay shades his face. Then a handicapped runner for the 6.15 crashes violently against him in avoiding a platoon of soldiers, and knocks his hat over his eyes and his stick ten yards away. When the great big world ceases turning and he finds a voice, the offender has gone. The next glance he shoots at the clock is choleric. A slight prod from an old lady who wishes to find the main booking-office produces a spout of fury; and the comedy ends with a gestic departure, in the course of which he gets a little of his own back on other of his species. His final glance at the clock is charged with the pure essence of malevolence.

How much more gracious is an appointment in the great resounding hall of Euston, though this is mainly a travellers' rendezvous and is seldom used for general appointments. Here, cloistered from the rush and roar of the station proper, yet always with a cheerful sense of loud neighbourhood, the cathedral mood is induced. You become benign, Gothic. There are pleasant straw seats. There are writing-tables with real ink. There are noble photographs of English beauty-spots, and —oh, heaps of dinky little models of railway trains and Irish Channel steamers which light up when you drop pennies in the slots. Vast, serene and episcopal is this rendezvous—it always reminds me of the Athenæum Club; and, however protracted your vigil, it showers upon you something of its quality; so that, though your friend be twenty minutes late, you still receive him affably, and talk in conversational tones of this and of that, instead of roaring the obvious like a baseball fan, as Victoria's hall demands. You may even make subtle epigrams at Euston, and your friend will take their point. I'd like to hear someone try to convey a fine shade of meaning in Victoria.

Oxford Circus Tube I register as the meeting-ground of the suburban flapper and the suburban shopping mamma. Its note is little swinging skirts, and artful silk stockings, and shining curls, that dance to the sober music of the matron's rustling satin. The waiting dames carry those dinky little brown-paper bags, stamped with the name of some Oxford Street draper, at whose contents the idler may amuse himself by guessing—a ribbon, a camisole, a flower-spray for a hat, gloves, or those odd lengths of cloth and linen which women will buy—though Lord knows to what esoteric use they put them. Hither come, too, those lonely people who, through the medium of " Companionship " columns or Correspondence Circles, have found a congenial soul. Why they choose Oxford Circus I don't know, but they are always to be seen there. You may recognize the type at first glance. They peer and scan closely every arrival, for, though correspondence has introduced them to the other soul, they have not yet seen the body, and they are searching for someone to fit the description that has been supplied; as thus: " I am of medium height and shall be wearing a black hat, trimmed with Michaelmas daisies, and a fawn macintosh," or " I am tall, and shall be wearing a grey suit and black soft hat and spectacles, and will carry a copy of the *Buff Review* in my hand." One is pleased to speculate on the result of the meeting. Is it horrible disillusion, or does the flint find its fellow-flint and produce the true spark? Do they thereafter look happily upon Oxford Circus Tube, or pass it with a shudder?

The crowd that hovers about the Leicester Square Tube entrances affords little matter for reflection. It is so obvious. It is so Leicester Square. It alternately snarls and leers. It never truly smiles; it is so tired of the smiling business. The loud garb of the women tells its own tale. For the rest, there are bejewelled black men, a few Australian and Belgian soldiers, and a few disgruntled and "shopless" actors. I never accept an appointment at Leicester Square Tube. It puts me off the lunch or dinner or whatever business is the object of the meeting. It is ignoble, squalid, with an air of sickly decency about it.

A few yards further Westward, at Piccadilly Tube, the atmosphere changes. One tastes the ampler ether and diviner air. It does not, like Charing Cross Post Office, sing April and May, but rather the mellowness of August and September. Good solid people meet here; people "comfortably off," as the phrase goes; people who have lived largely, but have not lost their capacity for deliberate enjoyment. At meal-times they gather thickly; quiet, dainty women; obese majors; Government officials; and that nondescript type that wears shabby, well-cut clothes with an air of prosperity and breeding. You may almost name the first words that will be spoken when a couple meet: "Well, where shall we go? Trocadero, Criterion—or Soho?" There is little hilarity; people don't "let themselves go" at this rendezvous. They are out for entertainment, but it is mild, well-ordered entertainment. The note of the crowd is, "If a thing is worth doing at all, it's worth doing well," even if the thing is only a hurried lunch or a curfew-rationed theatre. Classifying London's meeting-places by their moral atmospheres, I would mark Charing Cross Post Office as juvenile; Oxford Circus Tube as youth; Leicester Square Tube as senility; Piccadilly Tube as middle-age; the Great Hall at Euston as reverend seniority; and Victoria Station—well, Victoria Station should get a total-rejection certificate.

TRAGEDY AND COCKNEYISM

THE Cockney is popularly supposed to stand for the fixed type of the blasphemous and the cynical in his speech and attitude to life. He is supposed to jump with hobnailed boots on all things and institutions that are, to others, sacred. He is supposed to admit no solemnities, no traditional rites or services, to the big moments of life.

This is wrong. The Cockney's attitude to life is perhaps more solemn than that of any other social type, save when he is one of a crowd of his fellows; and then arises some primitive desire to mock and destroy. He will say " sir " to people who maintain their carriages or cars in his own district; but on Bank Holidays, when he visits territories remote from his home, he will roar and chi-ike at the pompous and the rich wherever he sees it.

But the popular theory of the Cockney is most effectively exploded when he is seen in a dramatic situation or in some moment of emotional stress. He does not then cry " Gorblimey " or " Comartovit" or some current persiflage of the day; or stand reticent and monosyllabic, as some superior writers depict him; but, from some atavistic cause, harks back to the speech of forgotten Saxon forefathers.

This trick you will find reflected in the melodrama and the cheap serial story that are made for his entertainment. It is hostile to superior opinion, but it is none the less true to say that melodrama does endeavour to reflect life as it is. When the wronged squire says to his erring son: "Get you gone; never darken my doors again," he is not talking a particular language of melodrama. He may be a little out of his part as a squire; that is not what a father of long social position and good education would say to a scapegrace son; but it is what an untaught town labourer would say in such a circumstance; and, as these plays are written for him, the writers draw their inspiration from his speech and manners. The programme allure of the Duke of Bentborough, Lord Ernest Swaddling, Lady Gwendoline Flummery, and so on, is used simply to bring him to the theatre. The scenes he witnesses, and the scenes he pays to witness, show himself banishing his son, himself forgiving his prodigal daughter, with his own attitudes and his own speech. The illiterate do not quote melodrama; melodrama quotes them.

Again and again this has been proved in London police-courts. When the emotions are roused, the Cockney does not pick his words and alight carefully on something he heard at the theatre last week; nor does he become sullen and abashed. He becomes violently vocal. He speaks out of himself. Although he seldom enters a church, the grip of the church is so tightly upon him that you may, as it were, see its knuckles standing in white relief when he speaks of solemn affairs. If you ask him about his sick Uncle John, he will not tell you that Uncle John is dead, or has "pegged out" or "snuffed it"; such phrases he reserves for reporting the passing of Prime Ministers, Dukes and millionaires. He will tell you that Uncle John has "passed away" or "gone home"; that it is a "happy release"; and, between swigs at his beer, he will give you intimate, but carefully veiled, details of his passing. He will never speak of the elementary, universal facts of life without the use of euphemism. A young unmarried mother is always spoken of as having "got into trouble." It is never said

TRAGEDY AND COCKNEYISM

that she is about to have a baby; she is "expecting." He never reports that an acquaintance has committed suicide; he has "done away with himself" or "made a hole in the water."

At an inquest on a young girl in the Bermondsey district, the mother was asked when last she saw her daughter.

"A'Monday. And that was the last time I ever clapped eyes on her, as Gawd is my witness."

At another inquest on a Hoxton girl, a young railwayman was called as witness. Having given his evidence, he suddenly rushed to the body, and bent over it, and cried loudly:—

"Oh, my dove, my dear! My little blossom's been plucked away!"

In a police-court maternity case, I heard the following from the mother of the deserted girl, who had lost her case: "Ah, God! an' shall this villain escape from his crime scot-free?" And in the early days of the war a bereaved woman created a scene at an evening service in a South London Church with this audible prayer: "Oh, Gawd, take away this Day of Judgment from the people, fer the sake of Thy Son Jesus. Amen."

Again, at Thames Police Court, during a case

of theft against a boy of seventeen, the father was called, and admitted to turning his son from home when he was fifteen, because of his criminal ways.

"Yerce, I did send 'im orf. An' never shall 'is foot cross my threshold until 'e's mended 'is evil ways."

The same reversion to passionate language may be found in many of the unreported incidents of battle. I have heard of Cockneys, whose pals were killed at their side, and of their comment on the affair in the stress of the moment:—

"Old George! I loved old George better'n I loved anything in the world. I'd 'ave give my 'eart's blood fer George."

And the cry of a mother at the Old Bailey, when her son was sentenced to death:—

"Oh, take me. Take my old grey 'airs. Let me die in 'is stead."—

And here is the extraordinary statement of a girl of fourteen, who, tired of factory hours and home, ran away for a few days, and then would not go back for fear of being whipped by her father. At the end of her holiday she gave herself up to the police on the other side of London from her home, and this was her statement to them:—

"Why can't I go where I want to? I don't do anybody any harm. I knew the world was good. I got tired of all the monotony, an' the same old thing every day, an' I wanted to get out. I am. Why bother me? I wonder why I can't go out and do as I like, so long as I don't do no harm. I thought the world was so big an' good, but in reality living in it is like being in a cage. You can't do nothing in this world unless somebody else consents."

Strange wisdom from a child of fourteen, spoken in moments of terror before uniformed policemen in that last fear of the respectable—the police-station. But it is in such official places that the Cockney loses the part he is for ever playing—though, like most of us, he is playing it unconsciously—and becomes something strangely lifted from the airy, confident materialist of his common moments. The educated man, on the other hand, brought into court or into other dramatic surroundings, ceases to be himself and begins to act. The Cockney, normally without dignity, achieves it in dramatic moments, where the man of position and dignity usually crumbles away to rubbish or ineptitude.

Hence, only the wide-eyed writers of melodrama have successfully produced the Cockney on the stage. True, they dress him in evening clothes, and surround him with impossible butlers and footmen, but if you want to probe the Cockney's soul, and cannot probe it at first-hand, it is to melodrama and the cheap serial that you must turn; not to the slum stories of novelists who live in Kensington or to the " low-life " plays of condescending dramatists.

MINE EASE AT MINE INN

WHEN everything in your little world goes wrong; when you can do nothing right; when you have cut yourself while shaving, and it has rained all day, and the taxis have splashed your collar with mud, and you receive an Army notice, post-marked on the outer covering *Buy National War Bonds Now*—in short, when you are fed up, what do you do?

To each man his own remedy. I know one man who, in such circumstances, goes to bed and reads Ecclesiastes; another who goes on an evening jag; another who goes for a ten-mile walk in desolate country; another who digs up his garden; another who reads school stories. But my own cure is to board a London tram-car bound for the outer suburbs, and take mine ease at a storied sixteenth-century inn.

Where is this harbour of refuge? No, thank you; I am not giving it away. I am too fearful that it may become popular and thereby spoiled. I will only tell you that its sign is " The Chequers"; that it is a low-pitched, rambling posthouse, with cobbled coach-yard, and ridiculous staircases that twist and wind in all directions, and rooms where apparently no rooms could be; that it was for a while the G.H.Q. of Charles the First; and that it is soaked in that ripe, substantial atmosphere that belongs to places where companies of men have for centuries eaten and drunken and quarrelled and loved and rejoiced.

You talk of your galleried inns of Chester and Shrewsbury and Ludlow and Salisbury, and your thousand belauded old-world villages of the West. . . . Here, within a brief tram-ride of London, so close to the centre of things that you may see the mantle of metropolitan smoke draping the spires and steeples, is a place as rich in the historic thrill as any of these show-places.

But its main charm for me is the goodly fellowship and comfortable talk to be had in the little smoking-room, decorated with original sketches by famous black-and-white men who make it their week-end rendezvous. You may be a newcomer at "The Chequers," but you will not long be lonely unless your manner cries a desire for solitude. Its rooms are aglow with all those little delights of the true inn that are now almost legendary. One reads in old fiction and drama of noble inns and prodigally hospitable landlords; but I have always found it difficult to accept these pictures as truth. I have sojourned in so many old inns about the country, and found little welcome, unless I arrived in a car and ordered expensive accommodation. It was not until I spent a night at "The Chequers" that I discovered an inn that might have been invented by Fielding, and a landlord who is and who looks the true Boniface.

I had missed the last car and the last train back to town. I wandered down the not very tidy High Street, and called at one or two of the hundred taverns that jostle one another in the street's brief length. The external appearance of "The Chequers" promised at least a comfortable bed, and I booked a room, and then wandered to the bar. I felt dispirited, as I always do in inns and hotels; as though I were an intruder with no friend in the world. I ordered a drink and looked round the little bar. My company were a police-sergeant in uniform, a horsey-looking man in brown gaiters, an elderly, saturnine fellow in easy tweeds, a young fellow in blue overall—obviously an electrician's mechanic—and a little, merry-faced chap with a long flowing moustache. I scrutinized faces, and sniffed the spiritual atmosphere of each man. It was the usual suburban bar crowd, and I assumed that I was in for a dull time. The talk was all saloon-bar platitudes—*This was a Terrible War. The rain was coming down, wasn't it? Yes, but the farmers could do with it. Yes, but you could have too much of a good thing, couldn't you? Ah, you could never rely on the English climate. . . . Three shillings a pound they were. Scandalous. Robbery. Somebody was making some money out of this war. Ah, there was a lot going on in Whitehall that the public never heard about. . . .* So, clutching at a straw, I opened the local paper, and read about A Pretty Wedding at St. Matthew's, and a Presentation to Mr. Gubbins, and a Runaway Horse in the High Street, and a——

Then came the felicitous shock. From the horsey man came words that rattled on my ears like the welcome hoofs of a relief-party.

"No, it wasn't Euripides, I keep telling you. It was Sophocles," he insisted. "I know it was Sophocles. I got the book at home—in a translation. And I see it played some time ago in town. Ask Mr. Connaught here if I'm not right." He grew flushed as he argued his rightness. I followed the direction of his nod. Mr. Connaught was the disgruntled-looking man in tweeds. And Mr. Connaught set down his whisky, fished in a huge well of a side-pocket, and produced— *Œdipus Rex* in the original Greek, and began to talk of it.

I sank back, abashed at my too previous judgment. Here was a man who, during the half-hour that I had been sitting there, had talked like a grocer or a solicitor's clerk—of the obvious and in the obvious way. It was he who had made the illuminating remarks that there was a lot going on in Whitehall that we didn't know anything about, and that you could never rely on the English climate. And now he was raving about Sophocles, and chanting fragments to the assembled whisky-drinkers. Tiring of Sophocles, he dived again into the pocket and produced Aristophanes.

The talk then became general. The constable, apparently annoyed at so much Latin and Greek, thrust into the chatter a loud contention that when a man had finished with English authors, then was time enough to go to the classics. Give him

Boswell's *Johnson* and *Pepys' Diary* and a set of Dickens written in the language of his fathers, to keep on the dressing-table, within easy reach of the bed, like. The electrician's mechanic couldn't bother with novels; he was up to the neck just now in Spencer and Häckel and Bergson, and if we hadn't read Bergson, then we ought to: we were missing something. Then somehow the talk switched to music, and there followed a dissertation by the police-sergeant on ancient church music and the futility of grand opera, and names like Palestrina and Purcell and Corelli were thrown about, with a cross-fire of " Bitter, please, Miss Fortescue "—" Martell, please; just a splash of soda—don't drown it "—" Have you tried the beer at the 'Hole-in-the-Wall?'—horrible muck "—" Come on—drink up, there, Fred; you're very slow to-night."

" D'you know this little thing by Sibelius? " asked the merry fellow; and hummed a few bars from the *Thousand Seas*.

" Ah, get away with yer moderns! " snapped the police-sergeant. " This Debussy, Scriabine, Schonberg and that gang. Keep to the simplicities, I say—Handel, Bach, Haydn and Gluck. Listen to this; " and he suddenly drew back from the bar, lifted a mellow voice at full strength, and delivered "Che Faro" from *Orfeo;* and then took a mighty swig at a pint tankard and said that it had just that bite that you only get when it's drawn from the wood.

It took me some time to pull myself together and sort things out. I wondered what I had stumbled upon: whether other pubs in this suburb offered similar intellectual refreshment; whether all the local tradesmen were bookmen and music-lovers; and how to reconcile the dreary talk that I had first heard with the enthusiastic and individual discourse that was now proceeding. I wondered whether it were a dream, and how soon I should wake up. If it were real, I wondered if people would believe me if I told them of it.

But soon I dismissed all speculation, for by a happy chance I was drawn into the circle. Some discussion having arisen on beer and its varying quality, a member of the company produced a once-popular American pamphlet, entitled *Ten Nights in a Bar-Room;* whereupon I handed round a little brochure of my own, compiled, for private circulation, from contributions by members of that London rambling Club, "The Blueskin Gang," and entitled *Ten Bar-Rooms in a*

Night. This pleased the company, and I at once became popular and had to take my part in the gigantic beer-drinking. Then the merry-faced little fellow slipped away, and quickly returned to counter my move with an old calf-bound seventeenth-century book, *The Malt-Worm's Guide:* a description of the principal London taverns of the period, with notes as to the representative patrons and the quality of the entertainment, material and moral, offered by each establishment; every page adorned with preposterous but captivating woodcuts.

On my suggesting that " The Blueskin Gang " might compile a similar guide on the London bars of to-day, each member of the company burst in with material for such a work. We decided that it would be impossible to follow the model of *The Malt-Worm's Guide* for such a work, since the London taverns of to-day are fast shedding their individual character. Formerly, one might know certain houses as a printers' bar, a journalists' bar, a lawyers', and so on. The " Cock," in Fleet Street, remains a rendezvous for legal gentry, and the taverns between Piccadilly and Curzon Street are still "used" by grooms and butlers; and two Oxford Street bars are the unregistered headquarters of the furniture trade. And do you know the "Steam Engine" in Bermondsey, the haunt of the South-Eastern Railway men, where gather engine-drivers, firemen, guards and other mighty travellers? A pleasant house, with just that touch of uncleanliness that goes with what some people call low company, and produces a harmony of rough living that is so attractive to matey men. And the Burton they used to sell in old times—oh, boy—as my American friends say—even to think of it gives you that gr-rand and gl-lor-ious feelin'.

But these places make the full list. The war has largely obliterated fine distinctions. The taverns of the Strand and its side streets, once the clubs of the lower Thespians, have become the rendezvous of Colonial soldiers. The jewellers who once foregathered at the Monico, have been driven out by French and Belgian military; and Hummum's, in Covent Garden, into which you hardly dared enter unless you were a market-man, has become anybody's property.

While I named the taverns of central London and their pre-war character, others of the company threw in details of obscure but highly-flavoured houses in outlying quarters of the city to which their business had at times occasioned them, with much inside information as to the special drinks of each establishment and its regular frequenters. I saw at once that such a work, if produced, would exceed the bulk of Kelly's Post Office Directory, but the discussion, though of no practical value, gave me a closer view of the idiosyncrasies of the company. The lover of Sophocles liked loud, jostling bars, reeking with the odour of crowded and violent humanity, where you truly fought for your drink; where no voice could be heard unless your ear were close upon it, and where you had barely room to crook your elbow: such bars as you find in the poorer quarters, as seem, at first acquaintance, to be under the management of the Sicilian Players. The electrician preferred a nice quiet house where he could sit down—no doubt to think about Bergsonism. The musical police-sergeant had no preferences in the matter of company or surroundings; the quality of the beer was all his concern. The horsey-looking man liked those large, well-kept, isolated suburban bars where you might find but two or three customers with whom you could have what he called a Good Old Talk About Things.

At closing time I discovered that the little merry-faced fellow was the host; indeed, I had placed him in some such capacity, for his face might have been preserved on canvas as the universal type of the jovial landlord.

"You're staying here, aren't you? Come through to my room for a bit. Unless you want to get off to bye-bye."

I didn't want to get off to bye-bye. I wanted to know more of this comic-opera inn. So I followed him to his private room, and I found it walled with books—real books, such as were loved by Lamb—*The Anatomy of Melancholy*, Walker's *Original*, *The Compleat Angler*, an Elizabethan Song-book, Descartes, Leopardi, Montaigne, and so on. The piano in the corner bore an open volume of Mozart's Sonatas; and this extraordinary Boniface, having "put the bar up," seated himself and played Mozart and Beethoven and Schumann and Isolde's "Liebestod," and morsels of Grieg, until three o'clock in the morning, when I climbed to my room.

On the way he showed me the King Charles room and the delightful eighteenth-century mezzotints on the stair-case walls, and the secret way from the first floor to the yard. From that night our friendship began. I stayed there the following day and for two days more, and pulled his books about, and roamed over the many rooms, and met the company of my first night in the bar.

I was charmed by the air of intimacy that belongs to that bar, deriving, I think, from the sweet nature of the host. You may stay at popular inns or resplendent hotels, and make casual acquaintance in the lounges, and exchange talk; but it is impossible, in the huge cubic space of such establishments, to come near to other spirits. You do not meet a man in town and say: "What? You've stayed at the 'Royal York'? I've stayed there too," and straightway develop a friendship. But you can meet a stranger, and say: "What? You know 'The Chequers?' D'you know Jimmy?" and you fall at once to discussing old Jimmy, the landlord, and you admit the stranger to the secrets of your heart.

Jimmy—I hope he won't mind my writing him down as Jimmy; you have only to look at him to know that he cannot be James or Jim—Jimmy radiates cheer; whether in his own inn or in other people's. Among his well-smoked furniture and walls men talk freely and listen keenly. There is no obscene reticence, no cunning reserve. Unpleasant men would be miserable at "The Chequers"; they would seek some other biding-place where self-revelation is kept within diplomatic bounds.

Believe me, " The Mermaid " was not the end of the great taverns. What things have we seen done and heard said at the bar of "The Chequers." What famous company has gathered there on Sunday evenings, artists, literary men, musicians, philosophers, entering into fierce argument and vociferous agreement with the local stalwarts. In these troubled times people are mentally slack. They readily accept mob opinion, to save themselves the added strain of thinking; and eagerly adopt the attitude that it is idle to concern oneself with intellectual affairs in these days; so that there is now no sensible talk to be had in bar or club. Wherefore, it is a relief to possess one place—and that an inn—where one may be sure of finding company that will join with relish in serious talk and put their whole lives in a jest. Such delight and refreshment do I find at this inn, that scarcely a Saturday passes but I board the car and glide to " The Chequers " in—well, just beyond the London Postal District.

RELICS

THE turning-out of the crowded drawers of an old bureau or cabinet is universally known as the prime pastime of the faded spinster; a pastime in which the starved spirit may exercise itself among delicious melancholies and wraiths of spent joys. Well, I am not yet faded, and I am not a spinster; but I have fallen to the lure of " turning out." I have lately " turned out "—not the musty souvenirs of fifty years ago, love, fifty years ago, but the still warm fragments of A.D. 1912.

The other day, while searching irately in my fumed-oak rolltop desk for a publisher's royalty statement which he had not sent me, I opened at random a little devil of a drawer who conceals his being in the right-hand lower corner. And lo! out stepped, airily, that well-polished gentleman, Mr. Nineteen-Twelve. My anger over the missing accounts was at once soothed. In certain chapters of this book I have harked back to the years before 1914, and it may be that you conceive me as a doddering old bore: a praiser of times past. But what would you have? You have not surely the face to ask me to praise times present?

So I took a long look at Mr. Nineteen-Twelve, and went thoroughly through him. My first discovery was an old menu. My second discovery was a bunch of menus. You won't get exasperated—will you?—if I print here the menu of a one-and-sixpenny dinner, eaten on a hot June night in Greek Street:—

Hors-d'œuvre varié.

. .

Consommé Henri IV.
Crème Parmentier.

. .

Saumon bouillé.
Concombre.

. .

Filet mignon.
Pommes sautés.
Haricots verts.

. .

Poulet en casserole.
Salade saison.

. .

Fraises aux liqueurs.
Glace vanille.

. .

Fromages.

. .

Dessert.

. .

Café.

I dug my hand deeper into the pockets of Mr. Nineteen-Twelve, and menu after menu and relic after relic came forth. There was a menu of a Lotus Club supper. I'm hanged if I can remember the Lotus Club, or its idea, or even its situation. There were old hotel bills, which, thrown together in groups, might suggest itineraries for some very good walking tours; for there were bills from Stratford-on-Avon and Goring-on-Thames and High Wycombe and Oxford and Banbury; there were bills from Bognor and Arundel and Chichester and the Isle of Wight; there were bills from Tintern and Chepstow and Dean Forest and Monmouth; there were bills from Kendal and Appleby and Windermere and Grasmere. Another clutching hand gave up old menus from the Great Western, the North-Western, and the Great Northern dining-cars. In a corner I found an assortment of fancy cigarette tins and boxes, specially designed and engraved for various restaurants and hotels. Now the cigarette tins are no more, and the boxes are made from flimsy card and are none too well printed, and many of the restaurants from which they came have disappeared, these elaborate productions are treasurable, not only as echoes of the good days, but as *objets d'art*.

Further search produced a flat aluminium match-case containing twelve vestas, and crested "With compliments—Criterion Restaurant"; and a tin waistcoat-pocket match box, also full, containing, on the inside of the lid, a charming glimpse of the interior of the Boulogne Restaurant—a man and woman at table, in 1912 fashions, lifting champagne glasses and crying, through a loop that begins and finishes at their mouths: "*Evviva noi!*" The sight of this streak of matches spurred me to further prospecting, and the pan, after careful washing, yielded boxes from Paris, with gaudy dancing-girls on either cover; insanely decorated boxes from Italy, filled with red-stemmed, yellow-headed matches; plain boxes from Monaco; and from Ostend, very choice boxes, decorated inside and outside with examples of the Old Masters.

Packets of toothpicks, with wrappers advertising various English and Continental bars, came from another corner, where they were buried under a torn page from an old *Tatler*, showing, in various phases, Portraits of a Well-Dressed Man.

This species being now extinct, I hope the plate of that page has been destroyed, so that my relic may possess some value. Two tickets for the Phyllis Court enclosure at Henley lay neglected under a printed invitation to have " A Breath of Fresh Air with the ' Old Mitre ' Christmas Club, Leaving the ' Old Mitre ' by four-horse brake at 10.30, to arrive at ' The Green Man,' Richmond, at 12 noon. A Whacking Good Dinner and a Meat Tea. Dancing on the Lawn at Dusk." An old programme of the Covent Garden Grand Season recalled that magnificent band of Wagnerians, Knupfer, Dittmar, van Rooy and the rest. Where are they now—these bull-voiced Rhinelanders? Within the programme covers I found a ticket for admission to the fight between young Ahearn and Carpentier which was abandoned; a printed card inviting me to a Tango Tea at the Savoy; a request for the pleasure of my company at the Empress Rooms to dance to the costive cacophony of a Pink Bavarian Band; and half a dozen newspaper cuttings, with scare-heads and cross-heads, dealing at much length with Debussy's tennis-court ballet, " Jeux," danced by Nijinsky, Schollar and Karsavina. Turning over one of these cuttings, I found a long report of the

RELICS

burning of a pillar-box by a Suffragette, and a list of recent window-breakings.

A little packet at the bottom caught my eye, and I dived for it. It was a small box of liqueur chocolates from Rumpelmayer's—unopened, old boy! unopened. I am a devil for sweets, and I was beginning to tear the wrapper, when conscience bade me pause. Ought I to eat them? Ought I not first to ascertain whether there were not others whose need was greater than mine? Think of the number of girls who would give their last hairpin for but one of the luscious little umber cubes. What right had I to liqueur chocolates of 1912 vintage? Conscience won. The packet is still unopened; and if, within seven days from the appearance of these lines, the ugliest girl in the W.A.A.C. will let me have her name and address and photograph, it will be sent to her. Failing receipt of any application by the specified date, I shall feel free to eat 'em.

Two others relics yet remained. One was a small gold coin, none too common, even in those days, and now, I believe, obsolete. I fancy we called it a half-sovereign, or half-quid, or half-thick-un or half-Jimmy, according to the current jargon of our set. The other was a throw-away leaflet, advertising on one side the programme of a London County Council concert in Embankment Gardens, and on the other the cheap Sunday and Monday excursions arranged by the National Sunday League.

This was the most heart-breaking of all the mementoes. How many Sundays, that otherwise might have been masses of melancholy, were shattered into glowing fragments by these inexpensive peeps at the heart of England? I can remember now these fugitive glimpses, with every little incident of each glad journey; and I am impelled to breathe a prayer from the soul for the well-being of the Sunday League, since it was only by the enterprise of the kindly N.S.L. that I was able to see my own country. Here I give you the list of trips, with return fares, advertised on the leaflet before me:—

	s.	d.
Brighton	2	6
Hastings	3	0
Eastbourne	4	0
Sheffield	5	0
Leeds	5	0
Weston-super-Mare	4	0
Tintern Abbey	4	6
Stratford-on-Avon	4	0
Warwick	4	0
Bournemouth	5	0
Isle of Wight	6	0

RELICS

Cardiff	5	0
Shrewsbury	4	6
Margate	3	6
Herne Bay	3	0
Cromer	5	0
Durham	6	0
York	5	0

Sacred name of an Albert Stanley!

Uttering this ejaculation, I restored my treasures to their hiding-place with the fumbling fingers of the dew-eyed, ruminative spinster, and locked the drawer against careless hands; hoping that, some day, some keen collector of the rare and curious might come along and offer me a blank cheque for this collection of Nineteen-Twelviana. Looking it over, I consider it a very good Lot—well-assorted; each item in mint state and scarce; one or two, indeed, unique.

What offers?

ATTABOY!

ON a bright afternoon of last summer I suffered all the thrills described in the sestet of Keats's sonnet, "On First Looking Into Chapman's Homer." I discovered a new art-form. I felt like that watcher of the skies. I stood upon a peak in Darien. But I was not silent, for what I had discovered was the game of baseball, and —incidentally—the soul of America.

That match between the American Army and Navy teams was my first glimpse of a pastime that has captivated a continent. I can well understand its appeal to the modern temperament; for it is more than a game: it is a sequence of studied, grotesque poses through which the players express all the zest of the New World. You should see Williams at the top of his pitch. You should see the sweep of Mimms' shoulders at the finish of a wild strike. You should see Fuller preparing to catch. What profusion of vorticist rhythms! With what ease and finish they were executed! I know of no keener pleasure than that of watching a man do something that he fully knows how to do—whether it be Caruso singing, Maskelyne juggling, Balfour making an impromptu speech, a doctor tending a patient, Brangwyn etching, an engineer at his engines, Pachmann at the piano, Inman at the billiard-table, a captain bringing his ship alongside, roadmen driving in a staple, or Swanneck Rube pitching. Oh, pretty to watch, sir, pretty to watch! No hesitation here; no feeling his way towards a method; no fortuitous hair's-breadth triumph over the nice difficulty; but cold facility and swift, clear answers to the multiple demands of the situation. Oh, attaboy, Rube!

I was received in the Army's dressing-room by Mimms, their captain, who said he was mighty glad to know me, and would put me wise to anything in the game that had me beat. The whole thing had me beat. I was down and out before the Umpire had cried his first "Play Ball!" which he delivered as one syllable: "Pl'barl!" The players in their hybrid costumes—a mixture of the jockey and the fencer—the catcher in his gas mask and stomach protector and gigantic mitt, and the wild grace of the artists as they "warmed up," threw me into ecstasy, and the new thrill that I had sought so long surged over my jaded spirit.

Then the game began, and the rooting began. In past years I attended various Test Matches and a few football matches in Northern mining districts, when the players came in for a certain amount of barracking; but these affairs were church services compared with the furious abuse and hazing handed to any unfortunate who made an error. Such screams and eldritch noises I never thought to hear from the human voice. No Englishman could achieve them: his vocal cords are not made that way. There was, for example, an explosive, reverberating "*Ah-h-h-h-h-h!*" which I now practise in my backgarden in order to scare the sparrows from my early peas. But my attempts are no more like the real thing than Australian Burgundy is like wine. I can achieve the noise, but some subtle quality is ever lacking.

The whole scene was barbaric pandemonium: the grandstand bristling with megaphones and tossing arms and dancing hats and demoniac faces offered a superb subject for an artist of the Nevinson or Nash school. A Chinese theatre is but a faint reflection of a ball game. I had never imagined that this hard, shell-covered, business people could break into such a debauch of frenzy. You should have heard the sedate Admiral Sims, when the Navy made a homer, with his : "Attaboy! Oh, attaway to play ball! Zaaaa. Zaaa. Zaaa!" and when his men made a wild throw he sure handed them theirs.

Here are a few of the phrases hurled at offending players:—

"Aw, well, well, well, well, well!"

"Ah, you pikers, where was you raised?"

"Hey, pitcher, is this the ball game or a corner-lot game?"

"Say, bo, you *can* play ball—maybe."

"Hey, catcher, quit the diamond, and lemme li'l brudder teach yeh."

"Say, who's that at bat? What's the good of sending in a dead man?"

"Aw, dear, dear, dear! Gimme some barb' wire. I wanter knit a sweater for the barnacle on second."

"Oh, watch this, watch this! He's a bad actor. Kill the bad actor!"

"More ivory—more ivory! Oh, boy, I love every bone in yer head."

"Get a step-ladder to it. Take orf that pitcher. He's pitching over a plate in heaven."

"Aw, you quitter. Oh. Oh. Oh. Bonehead, bonehead, bonehead. *Ahhhh.*"

"Now show 'em where you live, boy. Let's have something with a bit of class to it."

"Give him the axe, the axe, the axe."

"What's the matter with the man on third? 'Tisn't bed-time yet."

An everlasting chorus, with reference to the scoring-board, chanted like an anthem:—

"Go-ing up! Go-ing up! Go-ing up!"

At the end of the game—the Navy's game all the way—the fury and abandon increased, though, during the game, it had not seemed possible that it could. But it did. And when, limp and worn, I shuffled out to Walham Green, and Mimms asked me whether the game had got me, I could only reply, with a diminuendo:—

"Well, well, well, well, well!"

I shall never again be able to watch with interest a cricket or football match; it would be like a tortoise-race after the ball game. Such speed and fury, such physical and mental zest, I had never before seen brought to the playing of a simple game. It might have been a life-or-death struggle, and the balls might have been

Mills bombs, and the bats rifles. If the Americans at play give any idea of their qualities at battle, then Heaven help the fresh guys who are up against them.

When the boys had dressed I joined up with a party of them, and we adjourned to the Clarendon; where one of us, a Chicago journalist, not trusting the delicacy of the bartender's hand, obtained permission to sling his own; and a Bronx was passed to each of us for necessary action. This made a fitting kick to the ball game, for a Bronx is concentrated essence of baseball; full of quips and tricks and sharp twists of flavour; inducing that gr-r-rand and ger-l-lorious feelin'. It took only two of these to make the journalist break into song, and he gave us some excellent numbers of American marching-songs. He started with the American "Tipperary," sung to an air of Sullivan's :—

> Hail, hail, the gang's all here!
> What th'ell do we care?
> What th'ell do we care?
> Hail, hail, the gang's all here,
> So what th'ell do we care now?

Then "Happy-land" :—

> I wish I was in Happy-land,
> Where rivers of beer abound;

> With sloe-gin rickies hanging on the trees
> And high-balls rolling on the ground.
> What?
> High-balls rolling on the ground?
> Sure!
> High-balls rolling on the ground.

Then the anthem of the "dry" States:—

> Nobody knows how dry I am,
> How dry I am,
> How dry I am,
> You don't know how dry I am,
> How dry I am,
> How dry I am.
> Nobody knows how dry I am,
> And nobody cares a damn.

After this service of song, brief, bright and brotherly, we moved slowly Eastward, and in Kensington Gardens I learned something about college yells. For suddenly, without warning, one of the party bent forward, with arms outstretched, and yelled the following at a pensive sheep:—

"Alle ge reu, ge reu, ge reu. War-who-bar-za. Hi ix, hi ip; hi capica, doma nica. Hong pong. Lita pica. Halleka, balakah, ba."

At first I conjectured that the Bronx was running its course, but when he had spoken his piece the rest of the gang let themselves go, and I then understood that we were having a round of college yells. Respectable strangers might have mistaken the performance for the war march of the priests, or the entry of the gladiators, or the battle-song of the hairy Ainus; for such monstrous perversions of sense and sound surely have never before disturbed the serenity of the Gardens.

I understand that the essential of a good college yell is that it be utterly meaningless, barbaric and larynx-racking. It should seem to be the work of some philologist who had suddenly gone mad under the strain of his studies and had attempted to converse with an aborigine. I think Augustana's yell pretty well fills that condition:—

"Rocky-eye, rocky-eye. Zip, zum, zie. Shingerata, shingerata, bim, bum, bie. Zip-zum, zip-zum, rah, rah, rah. Karaborra, karaborra, Augus-*tana*."

At the conclusion of this choral service we caught a bus to Piccadilly Circus and I left them at the Tube entrance singing "Bob up serenely," and went home to dream of the ball game and of millions of fans screaming abstruse advice into my deaf ear.

Oh, attaboy!

* * * * *

Since that merry meeting I have had many opportunities of getting next to the American Army and Navy, and hearing their views of us and British views of them, and the experience has done me a lot of good. Until then, the only Americans I had met were the leisured, over-moneyed tourists, mostly disagreeable, and, as I have found since, by no means representative of their country. You know them. They came to England in the autumn, and stayed at opulent hotels, and made a lot of noise around ancient shrines, and sent local prices sky-rocketing wherever they stayed, and threw their weight and fifty-dollar tips about, and " Say'd " and " My'd " and " Gee'd " up and down the Strand; that kind of American. These people did their country a lot of harm, because I and thousands of other people received them as Americans and disliked them; just as wealthy trippers to and from other countries leave bad impressions of their people. I made up my mind on America from my meetings with these parvenus. I had forgotten that the best and typical people of a country are the hard-working, stay-at-home people, whose labours just enable them to feed and clothe their children and provide nothing for gadding about to other countries. To-day, the solid middle-class people of England and America are meeting and mixing, and all political history is washed out by the waters of social intercourse between them. High officials and diplomats are for ever telling one another over official luncheon tables that the friendship of this and that nation is sealed, but such remarks are valueless until the common people of either country have met and made their own decision; and the cost of living does not permit such meetings. Thus we have wars and unholy alliances. If only the common people of all countries could meet and exchange views in a common language, without the prejudice inspired by Press and politician, international amity would be for ever established, as Anglo-American amity is now established by the free-and-easy meeting of hard-working, middle-class Americans and the same social type of Englishman.

After meeting hundreds of Americans of a class and position similar to my own, I have changed all my views of America. We have everything in common and nothing to differ about. I don't care a damn on whose side was right or wrong in 1773. I have taken the boys round London. I have played their games. I have eaten their food. I have talked their slang and taught them mine. They have eaten my food, and we have sported joyfully together, and discussed music and books and theatres, and amiably amused ourselves at the expense of each other's social institutions and ceremonies. As they are guests in England, I have played host, and, among other entertainment that I have offered, I have been able to give them what they most needed; namely, evenings and 'odd hours in real middle-class English homes, where they could see an Englishwoman pour out tea and see an English baby put to bed. I found that they were sick of the solemn " functions " arranged for their entertainment. They didn't want high-brow receptions or musical entertainments in Mayfair. They preferred the spontaneous entertainment arising from a casual encounter in the street, as by asking the way to this or that place, leading to an invitation to a suburban home and a suburban meal. From such a visit they get an insight into our ways, our ideals, our outlook on life, better than they ever could from a Pall Mall club or a Government official's drawing-room. They get the real thing, which is something to write home about. In the " arranged " affairs they are "guests"; in the others, they are treated with the rude, haphazard fellowship which we extend to friends.

In these troubled days there is little room for the exercise of the graces of life. Our ears are deaf to the gentle voice of urbanity. The delicacies of intercourse have been trodden underfoot, and lie withered and broken. Even the quality of mercy has been standardized and put into uniform. Throughout the world to-day, everything is organized, and to organize a beautiful movement or emotion is to brutalize it: while lubricating its mechanism you ossify its soul. Thank God, there is still left a little spontaneity. Human impulse may be bruised and broken, but it is a fiery thing, and hard to train to harness or to destroy; and I can assure you that the Americans are grateful for it wherever it finds expression.

One evening, just before curfew—it was night according to the Government, but the sky said quite clearly that it was evening—I was standing at my favourite coffee-stall near King's Cross, eating hard-boiled eggs and drinking introspective coffee, and chatting with the boss on the joy of life.

"Met any of the Americans?" I asked, anxious to get his opinion of them.

"Met any? Crowds of 'em."

"What do you think of 'em?"

"Oh, I dunno. Bit of a change after all these other foreigners. 'Strewth—d'yeh know, when a Cockney like yesself comes along to the stall I feel like dropping down dead—'strewth, I do. Never get none o' the usual 'appy crowd along now," he went on, mopping the sloppy counter.

"But how do the Americans strike you?"

"The Ameircans? Well . . ." He folded his arms, which with him is the flourish preliminary to an oration. Here is his opinion, which I think sums up the American character pretty aptly:—

"The Americans. Well, nice, likeable fellers I've alwis found 'em. Don't 'alf make for my stall when they come out o' the station. Like it better, they say, than Lady Dardy Dinkum's canteen inside. And cat.′. . . Fair clear me out every time they come. I get on with 'em top-'ole. There's something about 'em—I dunno what, some kind o' kiddishness—but not that exac'ly—a sort of——"

"Fresh delight in simple things," I suggested, drawing on my Pelmanized Bartlett.

"That's jest it. Mad about London, y'know. Why, I bin in London yers an' yers, and it don't worry me. Wants to know which is the oldest building in London, and where that bloke put 'is cloak in the mud for some Queen, an' where Cromwell was executed, and 'ow many generals is buried in Westminster Abbey. 'Ow should I know anything about Westminster Abbey? I live in Camden Town. I got me business t'attend to.

"There's a friend of mine, Mr. 'Ankin, the gentleman what takes the tickets at Baker Street —'e met two of 'em t'other day. Navy boys— from the country, I should think. D'you know, they spent the 'ole mornin' ridin' up and down the movin' staircase—yerce, and would 'ave spent the afternoon, too, on'y one of 'em tried to run up the staircase what was comin' down an' . . . Well, I dessay it was good practice for 'em, but, as Mr. 'Ankin told 'em, it's safer to monkey with a U-boat than with a movin' staircase. And anyway, 'e'll be out of hospital before 'is ship's moved.

"Yerce, I like the Americans—what I've seen of 'em. No swank about 'em, y'know—officers an' men, just alike, all pals together. Confidence. That's what they got. Talks to yeh matey-like—know what I mean—man to man kind o' thing. Funny the way they looks at England, though. I s'pose they seen it on the map and it looked smallish. One feller come round the stall t'other night, an' 'e'd got two days' leave an' thought 'e could do Stratford-on-Avon, Salisbury Cathedral, Chester, Brighton, Edinburgh Castle, an' the spot o' blood where that American gel, Marry Queener Scots, murdered 'er boy—all in two days. 'Ustle, I believe they calls it over there. So I told 'im to start 'ustlin' right away, else, when 'e got back, 'e'd find 'imself waiting on the carpet, waiting for the good old C.B. Likeable boys, though. 'Ere's to 'em. No, I'll 'ave a ginger-ale. I don't drink me own coffee—not when I'm drinkin' anyone's 'ealth, like. Well, *Attaboy,* as they say over there."